THEOLOGY
OF THE HUMAN
PERSON

Dr. Maxwell Shimba

Shimba Publishing LLC
Printed in the United States of America

First Printing Edition, 2023

Sometimes when we hear about another crime, we wonder, "What on earth was he/she thinking?" The impeccable fact is, many people have hardened their hearts, their thoughts have developed into a different belief system resulting in different thinking patterns, and these thoughts impacted the choices and actions that led to retribution or their incarceration. In this book, we will use the Bible to study some of the common beliefs and thoughts of people that have come out of a hardened heart, and match them up, one by one, with truths from the Infallible Word.

Table of Contents

Table of Contents

WHAT IS THE THEOLOGY
OF THE HUMAN PERSON?

Theology of the human person is a branch of theology that explores the nature, purpose, and significance of human beings from a religious or spiritual perspective. It often varies across different religious traditions, but some common themes include:

1. Creation: Many theological perspectives believe that humans are created by a divine being or force and are endowed with a special purpose or role in the world.

2. Image of God: In Christian theology, for example, humans are often seen as created in the image of God, which suggests a reflection of divine attributes such as reason, creativity, and moral consciousness.

3. Sin and Redemption: Many theological traditions also address the concept of human sinfulness and the need for redemption or salvation. This can involve discussions about human moral responsibility and the path to reconciliation with the divine.

4. Free Will: Theology often considers the role of free will in human decision-making and the moral implications of choices humans make.

5. Destiny and Afterlife: Theology of the human person frequently explores questions about the destiny of human souls, whether it be in an afterlife, reincarnation, or some other spiritual state.

6. Ethics and Morality: It often delves into the ethical and moral framework for human behavior, drawing from religious teachings and principles to guide human conduct.

It's important to note that the theology of the human person can vary widely between different religious traditions, such as

Christianity, Islam, Judaism, Hinduism, Buddhism, and others. Each tradition may have its own unique perspectives on these topics.

Guard Your Hearts:

Proverbs 4:23: Keep thy heart with all diligence; for out of it are the issues of life.

Whenever we hear about a crime on social media or read about it in the Newspaper, we are left flabbergasted and scratching our heads, wondering how on earth someone could have done such a heinous thing. For most of us, it is hard if not impossible to comprehend an urge to harm someone or steal something, especially if we consider the ramifications to the victim, their family, and ourselves.

Proverbs 23:7 says, "For as he thinketh in his heart, so is he." What we believe in our hearts affects our thinking, and what we think affects who we are and what we do.

Proverbs 4:23 says, "Keep thy heart with all diligence; for out of it are the issues of life." What is in our hearts becomes our thoughts. Our thoughts become our words, what we say becomes our actions, our actions turn into habits, our habits form our characters, and our characters shape our destinies.

The fact is, many people in the world today, have hardened their hearts, and their thoughts have developed into a different belief system resulting in different thinking patterns, and these thoughts impacted the choices and actions that led to their incarceration. In this book, we will be studying some of the common beliefs and thoughts that have come out of a hardened heart, and match them up, one by one, with truths from God's Word.

In contrast, this book isn't just for criminals - it's for everyone. If we're honest, we'll be able to see ourselves in some of these thinking errors, and we'll see someone we're counseling in other thinking errors. If we don't examine ourselves and listen to the nudging of the Holy Spirit, our hearts could become hardened, our thoughts set in stone, and we could change our own destinies with these same thinking errors.

1. In Mark 8:17-18, Jesus asked one question right after another. And His questions perfectly described the heart that is hardened. What symptoms did He highlight in His questions?

Mark 8:17-18

17 And when Jesus knew it, he saith unto them, why reason ye, because ye have no bread? perceive ye not yet, neither understand? have ye your heart yet hardened? 18 Having eyes, see ye not? and having ears, hear ye not? and do ye not remember?

a): Do you not yet perceive nor understand?

The disciples were concerned with their meager bread supply, and it was clear that each of them had forgotten how Jesus had just fed thousands with only a few loaves.

b): Is your heart still hardened?

c): Having eyes, do you not see?

Jesus confronted His disciples over their lack of understanding. From this we know that they could have done better than this. They could have understood more if they applied themselves more.

d): And having ears, do you not hear?

e): And do you not remember?

Questioning them as to the hardness of their hearts, Jesus spelled out for us the characteristics of this spiritual heart condition as an inability to see, understand, hear, and remember. Note how asking questions was one of Jesus' most commonly used tactics for teaching. If you watch for this (even highlight them), you will notice how often Jesus asks questions to make his point.

2. How did Paul describe the hardened heart in Ephesians 4:17-19?

Ephesians 4:17-19 KJV 17 This I say therefore, and testify in the Lord, that ye henceforth walk not as other Gentiles walk, in the vanity of their mind, 18 Having the understanding darkened, being alienated from the life of God through the ignorance that is in them, because of the blindness of their heart: 19 Who being past feeling have given themselves over unto lasciviousness, to work all uncleanness with greediness.

> a): that you should no longer walk as the rest of the
> Gentiles walk, in the futility of their mind
> b): having their understanding darkened,
> c): because of the ignorance that is in them,
> d): because of the blindness of their heart;
> e): have given themselves over to lewdness, to work all
> uncleanness with greediness.

Basically, the ignorance and lack of understanding of man is a heart problem. It is shown not only in a foolish denial of God, but also in his moral failures (licentiousness, uncleanness, greediness).

3. According to Proverbs 28:14, what will happen if we harden our hearts?

Proverbs 28:14 ¹⁴ Happy is the man that feareth always: but he that hardeneth his heart shall fall into mischief.

Sin causes hearts to grow hard, especially continual and unrepentant sin. Now we know that "if we confess our sins, God is faithful and just and will forgive us our sins" (1 John 1:9). However, if we don't confess our sins, they have a cumulative and desensitizing effect on the conscience, making it difficult to even distinguish right from wrong.

This sinful and hardened heart is tantamount to the "seared conscience" Paul speaks of in 1Timothy 4:1–2. Scripture makes it clear that if we relentlessly continue to engage in sin, there will come a time when God will give us over to our "debased mind" and let us have it our way.

4. Where do evil thoughts, murder, adultery, sexual immorality, theft, false witness, slander originate? (Matthew 15:19): heart

Matthew 15:19 KJV [19] For out of the heart proceed evil thoughts, murders, adulteries, fornications, thefts, false witness, blasphemies:

This reminds me of Proverbs 23:7: "For as a man thinketh in his heart, so is he." That is why it is so important to guard your heart. Proverbs 4:23–26 instructs believers to, "Above all else, guard your heart, for everything you do flows from it. Keep your mouth free of perversity; keep corrupt talk far from your lips. Let your eyes look straight ahead; fix your gaze directly before you. Give careful thought to the paths for your feet and be steadfast in all your ways."

5. God doesn't drive us to repentance … He leads us to repentance. However, according to Romans 2:5, what will happen if we harden our hearts and remain unrepentant?

Romans 2:5 KJV [5] But after thy hardness and impenitent heart treasurest up unto thyself wrath against the day of wrath and revelation of the righteous judgment of God;

In the first coming of Jesus the loving character of God was revealed with greatest emphasis. At the second coming of Jesus the righteous judgment of God will be revealed most clearly.

6. How is the hardened heart described in Isaiah 6:10? Make the heart of this people dull, And their ears heavy, And shut their eyes;

Isaiah 6:10 KJV [5] But after thy hardness and impenitent heart treasurest up unto thyself wrath against the day of wrath and revelation of the righteous judgment of God;

God told Isaiah to go and preach to a people who wouldn't respond, wouldn't hear, wouldn't understand the point … so that their guilt would be certain.

7. Read Mark 10:4-5. What precept did Moses write because of hardness in the hearts of the people of his time? Moses permitted a man to write a certificate of divorce, and to dismiss her.

Mark 10:4-5 KJV [4] And they said, Moses suffered to write a bill of divorcement, and to put her away. [5] And Jesus answered and said unto them, For the hardness of your heart he wrote you this precept.

The Mosaic law granting divorce was a concession to the hardness of their hearts. It was never commanded by God but permitted because of the hardness of the offending party (because of their unfaithfulness to their spouse). It was also permitted because of the hardness of the offended party (being unable to perfectly forgive and restore a damaged relationship).

8. According to James 2:15-16, what might be an indication of a hardened heart? When you do not help someone in need. Exhibit: "Depart in peace, be warmed and filled," but you do not give them the things which are needed for the body, what does it profit?

James 2:15-16 KJV [15] If a brother or sister be naked, and destitute of daily food, [16] And one of you say unto them, depart in peace, be ye warmed and filled; notwithstanding ye give them not those things which are needful to the body; what doth it profit?

We aren't saved by works … we are saved by grace through faith. BUT, faith without works is dead. Faith alone saves us, but you can tell if faith is real by checking to see if it is accompanied by works. Good works naturally follow faith, and if there are no good works … there may not be genuine saving faith.

9. One of the best examples of hardheaded hard-heartedness is found in the book of Exodus. Pharaoh refused to let the children of Israel leave the land of Egypt as God had commanded. The Bible mentions Pharaoh's heart being hardened 17 times. If this has

happened to you, what has God promised to do in Ezekiel 36:26 and Ezekiel 11:19?

Ezekiel 36:26 KJV 26 A new heart also will I give you, and a new spirit will I put within you: and I will take away the stony heart out of your flesh, and I will give you an heart of flesh.

Ezekiel 11:19 KJV 19 And I will give them one heart, and I will put a new spirit within you; and I will take the stony heart out of their flesh, and will give them an heart of flesh:

a): I will give you a new heart and put a new spirit within you;

b): I will take the heart of stone out of your flesh and give you a heart of flesh.

c): God will give them one heart, and He will put a new spirit within them,

d): God will take the stony heart out of their flesh, and give them a heart of flesh,

Hearts can also become hardened when we suffer setbacks and disappointments in life. No one is immune to trials here on earth. Yet, just as steel is forged by a blacksmith's hammer, so, too, can our faith be strengthened by the trials we encounter in the valleys of life. As Paul encouraged the Romans: "But we also rejoice in our sufferings because we know that suffering produces perseverance; perseverance, character; and character, hope. And hope does not disappoint us, because God has poured out His love into our hearts by the Holy Spirit, whom He has given us" (Romans 5:3–5).

10. What did God promise to do about their hearts in Jeremiah 24:7?

Jeremiah 24:7 KJV 7 And I will give them an heart to know me, that I am the LORD: and they shall be my people, and I will be their God: for they shall return unto me with their whole heart.

GOD will give them a heart to know Him, that He is the Lord;

11. How can you say that a person's heart is NOT hardened? (Ephesians 4:2-3 and 1 Peter 3:8):

Ephesians 4:2-3 ²With all lowliness and meekness, with longsuffering, forbearing one another in love;³ Endeavouring to keep the unity of the Spirit in the bond of peace.

1 Peter 3:8 KJV ⁸Finally, be ye all of one mind, having compassion one of another, love as brethren, be pitiful, be courteous:

a): Have all lowliness and gentleness, with longsuffering, bearing with one another in love,

b): endeavoring to keep the unity of the Spirit in the bond of peace.

c): having compassion for one another; love as brothers, be tenderhearted, be courteous;

12. Read 2 Chronicles 34:27 and 2 Kings 22:19. What happens to our prayers when God sees a tender, penitent, and humble heart?

God will hear and answer our prayers: Exhibit: I also have heard you," says the Lord.

2 Chronicles 34:27 KJV ²⁷Because thine heart was tender, and thou didst humble thyself before God, when thou heardest his words against this place, and against the inhabitants thereof, and humbledst thyself before me, and didst rend thy clothes, and weep before me; I have even heard thee also, saith the LORD.

2 Kings 22:19 KJV ¹⁹Because thine heart was tender, and thou hast humbled thyself before the LORD, when thou heardest what I spake against this place, and against the inhabitants thereof, that they should become a desolation and a curse, and hast rent thy clothes, and wept before me; I also have heard thee, saith the LORD.

God can heal any heart once we recognize our disobedience and repent of our sins. But true repentance is more than simply a resolute feeling of steadfast determination. Repentance manifests itself in a changed life.

After repenting of our sins, hard hearts begin to be cured when we study God's Word. If we are to live life to the fullest as God intended, we need to study and obey God's written Word, which not only keeps a heart soft and pure but allows us to be "blessed" in whatever we do (Joshua 1:8; James 1:25).

DR. MAXWELL SHIMBA

CHAPTER 1

IT IS ALL ABOUT
ME, ME, ME

"It's All About Me, Me, Me!"

Theology often provides valuable insights into addressing thinking errors characterized by extreme self-centeredness or egocentrism, where individuals perceive everything through the lens of "it is all about me, me, me." Such a perspective can be detrimental to both personal well-being and communal harmony. Theology encourages a shift in mindset by emphasizing the interconnectedness of all beings and the importance of empathy, compassion, and selflessness. Many religious traditions promote the idea that individuals are not isolated entities but part of a larger, interdependent whole, and this understanding can counteract the notion that everything revolves around the self.

Furthermore, theology offers a moral and ethical framework that challenges self-centered thinking by emphasizing values like altruism, service to others, and humility. In many theological teachings, selflessness is considered a virtue and a pathway to spiritual growth. Through reflection, prayer, and engagement with sacred texts, individuals can cultivate a deeper awareness of their place in the world and a more balanced perspective that recognizes the needs and concerns of others alongside their own. By embracing these theological principles, individuals can work to overcome the thinking error of excessive self-centeredness and foster a more harmonious and compassionate approach to life.

It's All About Me: But Is Narcissism A Disorder?

People with this thinking error tend to emphasize their total difference from and superiority to other people. They see themselves as special, peculiar, even "one of a kind."

Perhaps you heard this before, I don't care what you think. I don't care if you feel what I do is of concern to you. If you don't like it then you know what do. I am a grown woman; I can do whatever I want with my body. But then these same people will try to change everyone but themselves in order to get the results they say they want.

They use others to achieve their own ends. They are unable or unwilling to identify with or acknowledge other people's feelings. They simply cannot (or will not) relate to others' needs and desires. What they want or need is the thing that is most important in their own eyes, so they usually behave in a selfish and uncaring manner.

People with this thinking error are actually narcissists. The term originated from Greek mythology, where the young Narcissus fell in love with his own image reflected in a pool of water. Typical narcissists exhibit a pattern of traits and behaviors that signify infatuation and obsession with one's self to the exclusion of all others and the egotistic and ruthless pursuit of one's gratification, dominance and ambition.

"It's all about me syndrome" people are unlikely to generate close, warm, loving relationships. They are impatient, anxious or angry much the time. This has often been seen to result in abusive and dysfunctional relationships, loneliness, temper tantrums and provoking behavior leading to violence and domestic violence and murder, pornography and sexual fantasy addiction, alcohol and drug addiction, adultery, bankruptcy, divorce, child abuse, nervous breakdown and despair.

People who live under the "it's all about me" misconception will exaggerate their own achievements and talents to the point of lying. They see themselves as more competent than everyone else, and may attempt to assume a leadership position because of this - even though they do not yet have very many achievements under their own belt.

People with this thinking error are falling right in line with Satan's plan. He wants us to put ourselves first and others last. He loves to see us get "big heads" with inflated egos, and take for ourselves the glory that actually belongs to God. Just remember, but for the grace of God, we would be nothing. Any skills, talents and abilities we have were given to us by God and are to be used to glorify God, not ourselves. We have been put on earth to serve others, not ourselves.

Common types of narcissistic manipulation include:

- Triangulation. Someone using this tactic will try to pull a third person into your conflict, typically to reinforce their own opinion or position.

- Gaslighting. Someone trying to gaslight you try to get you to doubt your own perspective and reality, often by twisting facts or insisting things you remember didn't actually happen.

- Hoovering. This tactic involves attempts to reconnect, or pull you back into a toxic or abusive relationship.

- Silent treatment. This behavior becomes manipulative when someone purposely ignores you to control you or make you feel isolated.

- Scapegoating. Parents who use narcissistic manipulation may place all the blame on one child they designate as a scapegoat.

- Passive aggression. Indirect blame-shifting, sabotage, and sarcasm can all point to covert narcissistic manipulation.

These tactics can confuse you, make you question your sense of reality, and damage your self-esteem.

Narcissistic victim syndrome is a term that collectively describes the specific and often severe effects of narcissistic manipulation. While this isn't a recognized mental health condition, many experts acknowledge narcissistic abuse can have a serious, long-lasting impact on mental health.

1. Read Jeremiah 9:23-24

[23] Thus saith the LORD, Let not the wise man glory in his wisdom, neither let the mighty man glory in his might, let not the rich man glory in his riches: [24] But let him that glorieth glory in this, that he understandeth and knoweth me, that I am the LORD which exercise lovingkindness, judgment, and righteousness, in the earth: for in these things I delight, saith the LORD.

a) About what things would a carnal man be likely to boast? (vs. 23):
i): in his wisdom
ii): in his might
iii): in his riches
This is all pride - giving ourselves the credit for something that God has accomplished and taking the glory that belongs to God alone and keeping it for ourselves. Pride is essentially self-worship. Anything we accomplish in this world would not have been possible were it not for God enabling and sustaining us. "What do you have that you did not receive? And if you did receive it, why do you boast as though you did not?" (1 Corinthians 4:7). That is why we give God the glory—He alone deserves it.

b) If we're going to brag, what does the Lord say we should brag about? (vs. 24): That we understand and knows God, That He is the Lord, exercising lovingkindness, judgment, and righteousness in the earth. For in these He delight," says the Lord.

This phrase, "boast in the Lord," is also found in 1 Corinthians 1:31, where Paul, quoting Jeremiah 9:24, says, "Let the one who boasts boast in the Lord." True boasting in the Lord is actually boasting about His great attributes, boasting about what He has done for us, boasting about what He is still doing, and boasting about what He has promised to do.

2. 2 Corinthians 10:17-18

[17] But he that glorieth, let him glory in the Lord. [18] For not he that commendeth himself is approved, but whom the Lord commendeth.

Note: 2 Corinthians 10:17-18 is a direct quotation from Jeremiah 9:24. Here Paul was rebuking the Corinthian Christians who were bragging about him being the founder of their church. Paul said he could never boast about what he had accomplished in Corinth, since it was God who was at work through him.:

a) His only boast, therefore, could be ... (vs. 17: glory in the Lord.

b) In the end, who is it that is approved? (vs. 18): whom the Lord commends.

Paul wanted the respect of the Corinthian Christians, but he wanted it for their sake, not his own. He knew they were hurting their own spiritual growth and maturity by rejecting him. But as for himself, Paul was satisfied with the approval that came from the Lord.

This is the mindset where, especially those of us in ministry, must arrive. We tend to seek the approval of the people within our ministry – our co-workers and those that we serve. If someone criticizes or complains about us, we tend to feel discouraged. But we must continue in our work, no matter what others are saying. In the end, it is what God says about us that matters and will endure.

3. The only proper glorying for the believer is in God. It is God's commendation, not one's own or any other persons, that matters.:

Acts 12:21-22

²¹ And upon a set day Herod, arrayed in royal apparel, sat upon his throne, and made an oration unto them. ²² And the people gave a shout, saying, It is the voice of a god, and not of a man.

a) What did the people do in Acts 12:21-22 that was so offensive to God? the people kept shouting, "The voice of a god and not of a man!"

b) How did Herod, puffed up with pride and vanity, respond to their flattery? (vs. 23): he did not give glory to God.
Herod had a great time accepting all the praises and adulation, but his joy was short-lived.

c) What action did God take? (vs. 23): he was eaten by worms and died.

Think about it! The manner of Herod's death was appropriate to his spiritual state - he corrupted from the inside out.

d) Read Daniel 4:28-33. What infamous words, spoken by Nebuchadnezzar, brought about his downfall?

"Is not this great Babylon, that I have built for a royal dwelling by my mighty power and for the honor of my majesty?"

Nebuchadnezzar was considered the greatest king of the Babylonian Empire and is credited with the construction of the Hanging Gardens of Babylon. Nebuchadnezzar is best known for the conquering of Judah and the destruction of Judah and Jerusalem in 586 BC. Nebuchadnezzar is mentioned by name around 90 times in the Bible, receiving the most attention in the book of Daniel, appearing as the main character, beside Daniel, in chapters 1–4.

e) What happened to Nebuchadnezzar because he thought it was all about him?

That very hour the word was fulfilled concerning Nebuchadnezzar; he was driven from men and ate grass like oxen; his body was wet with the dew of heaven till his hair had grown like eagles' feathers and his nails like birds' claws.

f) Read on through the end of Daniel 4. Did Nebuchadnezzar ever break free from his madness?

According to the biblical account in the book of Daniel, Nebuchadnezzar, the Babylonian king, experienced a period of madness where he was driven out from human society and lived like a wild animal. However, the same account also states that Nebuchadnezzar eventually regained his sanity and his former position as king.

The book of Daniel describes how Nebuchadnezzar had a dream that troubled him and he sought interpretation from Daniel, a Jewish exile in Babylon. The dream prophesied that Nebuchadnezzar would lose his kingdom and his sanity if he did not acknowledge the power of God. Despite Daniel's warnings, Nebuchadnezzar refused to humble himself and instead boasted about his achievements, leading to his downfall.

After experiencing his period of madness, Nebuchadnezzar acknowledges the power of God and his kingdom is restored to him. He recognizes that God is the ultimate authority and humbles himself before Him. This is described in Daniel 4:34-37, where Nebuchadnezzar declares that God is "the King of heaven" and that "those who walk in pride he is able to humble."

It is worth noting that the historical accuracy of the biblical account of Nebuchadnezzar's madness has been a subject of debate among scholars, and there is no independent confirmation of this event outside of the Bible. However, the story of Nebuchadnezzar's humility and recognition of God's power has been an important lesson for many people throughout history.

g) Explain what happened next in Nebuchadnezzar's life.:

Nebuchadnezzar eventually praised God and his reason returned to him, and for the glory of his kingdom, his honor and splendor returned to him. His counselors and nobles resorted to him, he was restored to his kingdom, and excellent majesty was added to him.

The story of Nebuchadnezzar is an example of God's sovereignty over all men and the truth that "The king's heart is a stream of water in the hand of the Lord; He turns it wherever He will" (Proverbs 21:1).

4. Read Matthew 20:16. Matthew 20:16

¹⁶ So the last shall be first, and the first last: for many be called, but few chosen.

We may think it's all about us, and that we deserve to be the first one in line for whatever blessings God has to give out. But in this verse, Jesus said ...: So, the last will be first, and the first last. For many are called, but few chosen.

Heaven's value system is far different from earth's value system. And there will be many surprises when we get to heaven. But the Bible provides several examples by which we can already see how this holds true.

- Judas Iscariot was one of the first disciples and was honored to be the treasurer of the group, yet his greed led to his undoing;
- Paul was the last of the apostles (1 Corinthians 15:8–9) yet the one who worked the hardest (2 Corinthians 11:23).
- Based on the terms of the New Covenant, the Gentiles had equal access to the kingdom of heaven, although they had not served God under the Old Covenant. The Jews, who had labored long under the Old Covenant, were jealous of the grace extended to the Gentile "newcomers" (see Romans 11:11).
- There are some who are first in prestige and rank yet might never enter the kingdom.
- Jesus told the Pharisees that the sinners they despised were being saved ahead of them: "Truly I tell you, the tax collectors and the prostitutes are entering the kingdom of God ahead of you" (Matthew 21:31–32).

5. Much of this thinking error is rooted in pride. What does God say about pride?

a) James 4:6: "God resists the proud, But gives grace to the humble."

b) James 4:10: Humble yourselves in the sight of the Lord, and He will lift you up.

c) Philippians 2:3: Let nothing be done through selfish ambition or conceit, but in lowliness of mind let each esteem others better than himself.

d) Proverbs 16:19: Better to be of a humble spirit with the lowly, Than to divide the spoil with the proud.

There is a difference between the kind of pride that God hates (Proverbs 8:13) and the kind of pride we can feel about a job well done (Galatians 6:4) or the kind of pride we express over the accomplishment of loved ones (2 Corinthians 7:4). The kind of pride that stems from self-righteousness or conceit is sin, and God hates it because it is a hindrance to seeking Him.

6. What advice would you give a person operating under the "It's All About Me" thinking error?

The proverbial saying 'pride comes before a fall' is a warning that haughtiness and hubris leads to failure and loss. To choose pride is to set oneself up for a fall; the pedestal we make for ourselves proves a precarious foundation.

In other words, instead of being selfish and self-centered, making everything all about ourselves, we must strive to become SELFLESS. The characteristic of being selfless is one of the most important traits any Christian can have. It's so significant that Jesus said it is the second most important of all God's commandments: "You shall love your neighbor as yourself" (Mark 12:31; Galatians 5:14). Jesus wasn't creating a new law here; He was merely agreeing with and expounding on an Old Testament law (Leviticus 19:18). James calls this the "royal" law to emphasize its supreme value to God (James 2:8).

CHAPTER 2

WHAT IS MINE IS MINE. WHAT IS YOURS IS MINE TOO!

"What's Mine is Mine. What's Yours is Mine Too!"

Thinking errors, commonly known as cognitive distortions, are irrational beliefs that contribute to uncomfortable emotions and unwanted behavior. People with this thinking mentality may not be outspoken enough to say it out loud, but this is what they are really thinking. They think that what's theirs is theirs alone, but whatever is yours is theirs too – if they want it. They understand the concept of ownership, but they just feel that if they really want something – it should be theirs. And they don't think they should have to work to get it. If they don't get what they want, they believe they have been treated unfairly. If other people stand in the way of what they want, they presume they have the right to obtain it – by any means.

This way of thinking is connected with a person's mental attitude regarding the work ethic. Those with this mindset show no respect for the efforts, industry, and accomplishments of other people. They don't recognize boundaries. They have a spirit of entitlement – and if they want it, they will simply take it.

Society has contributed to this cognitive distortion thinking. What about the bankruptcy system that forgives our debts if we find ourselves in a financial bind? What about a government that seems to give public assistance forever to individuals and families? What about the medical care anyone can get when they walk into an emergency room, even when they don't pay? What about ministries that give food to the poor, but never really do anything to help them get of out the cycle of poverty?

If we're poor, we believe we deserve handouts from the government. If we're rich, we think we need a tax break. If we're employees, we want our employer to give us better benefits. If we're bankers, we apply for a bailout in tough times. If we're farmers, we expect subsidies. If we're a special interest group, we seek special treatment.

A big spiritual issue for people who feel the world owes them something is that they become dependent on the world to provide for their needs (and wants) instead of God. Another spiritual issue with this thinking error is covetousness.

One key to overcoming this thinking error is to develop a spirit of contentment. If we learn to be content with the blessings God has so graciously given to each one of us personally, we won't be looking at what everyone else has and finding ways to make what's theirs our own.

Covetousness, or greed, is forbidden several places in the Bible. Exodus 18:21, 1 Timothy 3:3, Titus 1:7, and 1 Peter 5:2 all say that hatred of covetousness is one qualification for leaders, both civil and religious. 1 Corinthians 5:11 tells us not to keep company with people who are covetous. In Ephesians 5:3, covetousness is named as one of six common sins that should not be named among the saints. And Colossians 3:5 reminds us that covetousness is idolatry.

1. Could you imagine the cultural revolution that would evolve in our country if people began to call anything God gave them beyond their basic necessities' "blessings" instead of "entitlements"?

1 Timothy 6:7-8

[7] For we brought nothing into this world, [a]and it is certain we can carry nothing out. [8] And having food and clothing, with these we shall be content.

a) What have we brought into this world? Nothing

b) What are we going to carry out of this world? Nothing

c) Today we have a constant hunger for more and more, better and better. What did Paul advise Timothy regarding this? And having food and clothing, with these we shall be content.

And a person should take time to enjoy the blessings and gifts that God has bestowed upon him.

A paradox of our times is that we spend more, but have less. We buy more, but enjoy less. We have bigger houses and smaller families. We have more conveniences but less time. We have multiplied our possessions but reduced our values. We've learned how to make a living, but not a life. We have more medicine but less wellness. Many homes today have two incomes but more marriages today end in divorce.

2. Read Hebrews 13:5-6.

[5] Let your conduct be without covetousness; be content with such things as you have. For He Himself has said, "I will never leave you nor forsake you." [6] So we may boldly say:

"The LORD is my helper; I will not fear. What can man do to me?"

Often covetousness and greed are excused or even admired in today's culture, and are simply called "ambition." Someone asked millionaire Bernard Baruch, "How much money does it take for a rich man to be satisfied?" Baruch answered, "Just a million more than he has.":

a) Hebrews 13:5a indicates that contentment includes freedom from covetousness.

Money and possessions can never satisfy us, because they do not address some of our most important needs. For example, we need loving relationships. Wealth cannot love, and indeed often interferes with our relationships with people and God.

b) When we are discontented and dissatisfied, one of the first thoughts that we might entertain is that God has abandoned us, that He does not care about us, that He has not blessed us. Why are we told we should be content? (vs. 5b): be content with such things as you have.

This promise was first made to Jacob in Genesis 28:15c, and is often repeated in the old and New Testaments. We find the promise was made to Joshua in Jos. 1:5. Again, this promise was given to Solomon in 1 Chron. 28:20, as one of David's last acts. What God did for them, He will do for you.

c) What will characterize a contented person? (vs. 6): When the Lord is my helper. Exhibit: The Lord is my helper; I will not fear.

This verse is actually taken from Psalm 118:6. To have the Lord on your side (Ps. 118:6) and taking your part (Ps. 118:7) is better than all the things men can buy with their money.

3. The discontented person seeks to fill the God-shaped vacuum within by acquiring things that he never satisfy. Read Ecclesiastes 5:10-20 for contentment clues.:

Ecclesiastes 5:10-20

[10] He who loves silver will not be satisfied with silver; Nor he who loves abundance, with increase. This also is vanity. [11] When goods increase, they increase who eat them; So what profit have the owners Except to see them with their eyes? [12] The sleep of a laboring man is sweet, Whether he eats little or much; But the abundance of the rich will not permit him to sleep. [13] There is a severe evil which I have seen under the sun: Riches kept for their owner to his hurt. [14] But those riches perish through [a]misfortune; When he begets a son, there is nothing in his hand. [15] As he came from his mother's womb, naked shall he return, to go as he came; And he shall take nothing from his labor, Which he may carry away in his hand. [16] And

this also is a severe evil— Just exactly as he came, so shall he go. And what profit has he who has labored for the wind? [17] All his days he also eats in darkness, And he has much sorrow and sickness and anger. [18] Here is what I have seen: It is good and fitting for one to eat and drink, and to enjoy the good of all his labor in which he toils under the sun all the days of his life which God gives him; for it is his heritage. [19] As for every man to whom God has given riches and wealth, and given him power to eat of it, to receive his heritage and rejoice in his labor—this is the gift of God. [20] For he will not dwell unduly on the days of his life, because God keeps him busy with the joy of his heart.

a) What did Solomon discover about money? (vs. 10): This also is vanity.

b) In what way did Solomon say riches interfere with a person's life?

According to Solomon, you are still working hard for more wealth, you have little disposable money because you spent it on more stuff, so your only benefit is to gaze with satisfaction on what you own.

i) vs. 12: the abundance of the rich will not permit him to sleep.

Here we see the contrast between the peace and contentment of the laboring man, and the unrest and sleeplessness of the rich man, whose lust for more money keeps him awake.

ii) vs. 13: Riches kept for their owner to his hurt.

iii) vs. 14: But those riches perish through misfortune; When he begets a son, there is nothing in his hand.

You may have noticed - covetousness becomes quite evident in three areas of a person's life.

1. In Getting: You will see that for this person acquiring wealth becomes the dominant passion of his soul. This might be the

workaholic, who works day and night to make more sales, bring in more money.

2. In Keeping. Such a person is a miser, clings to money as a drowning man to a log. There is a hoarding up for himself at the expense of others.

3. In Spending. As much as the covetous person is stingy with others, he is often reckless in spending on himself. Money which ought to be saved for a rainy day, is used to gratify his desires for unnecessary things.

c) To what is the attempt to accumulate compared?

(vs. 15-16): To vanity. Since you came with nothing and you shall go with nothing. As he came from his mother's womb, naked shall he return,

d) With a sympathetic touch, what does Solomon tells us may be the life even for those who have great wealth? (vs. 17): All his days he also eats in darkness, And he has much sorrow and sickness and anger.

e) What happens to the contented person according to verses 19-20?

He will rejoice in his labor. Exhibit: 19 As for every man to whom God has given riches and wealth, and given him power to eat of it, to receive his [c]heritage and rejoice in his labor—this is the gift of God. 20 For he will not dwell unduly on the days of his life, because God keeps him busy with the joy of his heart.

4. The Apostle Paul was forced to live in numerous places. Conditions and provisions varied greatly. He traveled back and forth between luxury and poverty. Study his comments in Philippians 4:10-20.:

Philippians 4:10-20

Philippian Generosity

[10] But I rejoiced in the Lord greatly that now at last your care for me has flourished again; though you surely did care, but you

lacked opportunity. [11] Not that I speak in regard to need, for I have learned in whatever state I am, to be content: [12] I know how to be abased, and I know how to abound. Everywhere and in all things, I have learned both to be full and to be hungry, both to abound and to suffer need. [13] I can do all things through Christ who strengthens me. [14] Nevertheless you have done well that you shared in my distress. [15] Now you Philippians know also that in the beginning of the gospel, when I departed from Macedonia, no church shared with me concerning giving and receiving but you only. [16] For even in Thessalonica you sent aid once and again for my necessities. [17] Not that I seek the gift, but I seek the fruit that abounds to your account. [18] Indeed I have all and abound. I am full, having received from Epaphroditus the things sent from you, a sweet-smelling aroma, an acceptable sacrifice, well pleasing to God. [19] And my God shall supply all your need according to His riches in glory by Christ Jesus. [20] Now to our God and Father be glory forever and ever. Amen.

a) Was Paul a naturally contented person?

Verse 11 tells us that Paul had to "learn" contentment. "Learn" means to acquire the knowledge by use and practice, to acquire the habit of, or to become accustomed to. We are also to "learn" to be angry and not sin. We have to learn not to make frustration, bitterness, and hostility regular parts of our lives.

b) List of the circumstances in which Paul learned to be content. (vs. 12):

i): I know how to be abased,

ii): and I know how to abound.

iii): Everywhere and in all things, I have learned both to be full

iv): and to be hungry,

v): both to abound

vi): and to suffer need.

I was struck by the words "I am instructed" in this verse. This instruction was given to Paul by the Holy Spirit. Oh, that we all would be as sensitive to the "instruction" of the Holy Spirit, as we encounter the variety of conditions that life brings. Our first response is usually to begin whining, so loudly that we can't hear the instructions.

c) Why was Paul able to adjust so easily? He could do all things through Christ who strengthens him.

The Bible tells us over and over that nothing is impossible through Jesus Christ. Matthew 17:20 tells us that, if we have faith, whatever we say will be done. Mark 9:23 teaches that, regardless of what it is or who it is, all things are possible providing there is unwavering faith.

"All things" spoken of in these verses refers to all things that pertain unto life and godliness. (2 Peter 1:3).

d) What did Paul say to encourage the Philippians who had sent gifts to him? (v. 19): God shall supply all their needs according to His riches in glory by Christ Jesus.

In this passage of scripture, Paul has actually hit upon the cure for worry and anxiety. Doctors, psychologists, and psychiatrist will go broke if the word gets out! Here are 10 cures for the person who worries.

1.	Permit the peace of God to keep your mind and heart through Jesus Christ. (Philippians 4:7)
2.	Renounce all worry and by prayer, supplication, and thanksgiving make all requests known to God. (Philippians 4:6)
3.	Think on right things. (Philippians 4:8)
4.	Keep your mind stayed on God. (Isaiah 26:3)
5.	Use the weapons of spiritual warfare. (2 Corinthians 10:4-6)
6.	Put on the whole armor of God. (Ephesians 6:10-18)
7.	Have faith in God. (Matthew 6:25-34)

8.   Live and walk in the Spirit. (Galatians 5:16-26)

9.   Do not cast away confidence. (Hebrews 3:6)

10. Cast all care upon God. (1 Peter 5:6-7)

Also, we should study His Word to find examples of contentment. The early Church certainly knew what it was to be content, and they serve as some of the greatest examples for us today. Oh, that we would all be free from care or worry because of satisfaction and contentment with what is already our own.

5. What advice would you give a person operating under the "What's Yours Is Mine" thinking error?

Is to develop a spirit of contentment. If we learn to be content with the blessings God has so graciously given to each one of us personally, we won't be looking at what everyone else has and finding ways to make what's theirs our own.

Praising God is another way to find more contentment - in spite of the problems that man can encounter. Singing our praises to God is even better, for the Lord inhabits the praises of His people.

Also, we should study His Word to find examples of contentment. The early Church certainly knew what it was to be content, and they serve as some of the greatest examples for us today. Oh, that we would all be free from care or worry because of satisfaction and contentment with what is already our own.

CHAPTER 3

IT IS MY WAY OR THE HIGHWAY

"It's My Way or the Highway."

The idiom 'my way or the highway' forcefully expresses the view that 'you can take it or leave it'. In fact, it really means 'take it or leave', as the highway refers to the road the listener should go down if they don't agree with the speaker. With the "it's my way or the highway" mentality, the person is suggesting an ultimatum to the listener(s) who may be family members, co-workers, or fellow inmates. If you're about to argue with a person with this mindset, the stakes can be high. What is implied is that you had better do exactly what they want or there will be severely negative consequences.

A person with this attitude is known for his/her stubbornness, unwillingness to listen or even compromise. This is usually the controlling, superior partner, the domineering boss, the close-minded father, the leader of the gang. Such a person is often wrong, but never doubts that he/she is correct. This person has preconceived notions, and can't be swayed to another way of seeing the situation. He/she has no respect for another person's opinion or life experience in similar situations. Such people are ready for a fight over every little thing, insisting that their position is the only position, and that their "right way" is the "only" right way?

Criminals need control and power over others. The need for power, control, and dominance shows up in every area of their lives. Their greatest power excitement comes from doing the forbidden and getting away with it.

The fact is - life is not always going to go our way, we are not always going to get our way, and the people who disagree with us are not always going to hit the highway. With this thinking error, it isn't what happens to or around criminals that makes them unhappy. It is their way of thinking about the events of their lives that makes them turn to violence or crime when things don't go their way, when everyone doesn't agree with them.

1. The theological truth about this lie can be found in Acts. 20:22-24. What was Paul's attitude, even though the Spirit had warned him that prison and hardships awaited him in every city?

We find that Apostle Paul was unmoved from the will of the Holy Spirit. Acts 20:22, the Apostle Paul began, "And now, behold, I go bound in the Spirit unto Jerusalem." Day after day Paul denied himself in order that he might walk in submission under the direction of God the Holy Spirit.

Paul didn't know what was ahead of him … he even had reason to believe it would be bad. But that didn't trouble him. He could give it all over to God even though he didn't know what would happen. We should ALL be willing to say, "None of these things move me. I will carry on with my assignment from God."

2. Read James 1:2-8.:

Profiting from Trials

[2] My brethren, count it all joy when you fall into various trials, [3] knowing that the testing of your faith produces patience. [4] But let patience have its perfect work, that you may be perfect and complete, lacking nothing. [5] If any of you lacks wisdom, let him ask of God, who gives to all liberally and without reproach, and it will be given to him. [6] But let him ask in faith, with no doubting, for he who doubts is like a wave of the sea driven and tossed by the wind. [7] For let not that man suppose that he will receive

anything from the Lord; ⁸ he is a double-minded man, unstable in all his ways.

a) What response did James recommend when things are not going our way? (vs. 2): count it all joy when you fall into various trials,

I'm in my 50's now, and I've been through a LOT of trials over the years – a couple that completely changed the direction of my life. But you know what I have discovered? God's joy really is there. You can consider each trial joy; you can greatly rejoice with joy inexpressible and full of glory … even when you feel like you have fallen face–down in the mud puddle. You can endure whatever circumstances are making you quake in your boots. And after the situation has passed, I can always find my "treasure of darkness" (Isaiah 45:3).

b) Why does he say this? (vs. 3-4): He was exhibiting that patience is the product of faith testing, and when the testing is finished, we will be complete "whole" while missing nothing. [3 knowing that the testing of your faith produces patience. 4 But let patience have its perfect work, that you may be perfect and complete, lacking nothing.]

How to face trials is the very first thing James writes about after his salutation. And the reason why is because of the importance of this topic. Many Christians think once they've made that decision for Christ that everything will fall into place and life will be that proverbial bowl of cherries. And when trials and tough times come upon new believers, sometimes they begin to question, "Why?"

c) How can a person handle the pressure in this situation? (vs. 5): By asking Wisdom from God. Exhibit: If any of you lacks wisdom, let him ask of God, who gives to all liberally and without reproach, and it will be given to him.

d) What enables a person to get help from God? (vs. 6): FAITH. Exhibit: But let him ask in faith, with no doubting, for he who doubts is like a wave of the sea driven and tossed by the wind.

Peter also tackles this issue of joy in the midst of trials in 1 Peter 1:6-9. James 1:2-8 clearly states that the testing of our faith produces perseverance. And the Peter passage states that our faith, which is priceless, will be proved genuine and result in praise to God.

3. Read Genesis 15:1-5 and then Genesis 16:1-16. Here we see what happens when someone insists on doing things "her way.":

a) What was Sarah's suggestion for helping God keep His promise? (vs. 1-3): Sarai said to Abram, "See now, the Lord has restrained me from bearing children. Please, go in to my maid; perhaps I shall obtain children by her." And Abram heeded the voice of Sarai.

To be childless in those days was considered a curse. Abraham was approximately 85 and Sarah was 76. They were both past the age when couples stopped having children. Sarah saw the hopelessness of her situation and proposed the use of a custom of the surrounding people. By assisting a concubine during childbirth, the wife could claim the child as her own. However, they would soon find out that this kind of adulterous behavior would not bring the happiness to the family that they hoped.

b) How did this alternate plan work out?

i) vs. 4: So, he went in to Hagar, and she conceived. And when she saw that she had conceived, her mistress became despised in her eyes.

ii) vs. 5: Then Sarai said to Abram, "My wrong be upon you! I gave my maid into your embrace; and when she saw that she had conceived, I became despised in her eyes. The Lord judge between you and me."

iii) vs. 6: So, Abram said to Sarai, "Indeed your maid is in your hand; do to her as you please." And when Sarai dealt harshly with her, she fled from her presence.

Now notice, this whole thing was Sarah's idea, not Abraham's, but Abraham got the blame - especially when he let Hagar go unpunished for her insolent and ungrateful conduct toward her mistress. (I know, you're thinking nothing has changed in all these years. The husband is always the one to get the blame when things go wrong!)

Abraham did not argue the point. He merely pointed out that Hagar is still Sarah's slave, and Sarah could punish her any way she pleased. Legally, Sarah could have killed Hagar because saves were considered property. Perhaps Abraham should have known that placing Hagar in the hands of his jealous wife would make matters even worse, but he was unaccustomed to handling this kind of situation. He compromised his morals again by knowingly placing someone in a dangerous position. He surprisingly shows little concern for his first, yet unborn, child.

c) Was Sarah's "way" or solution according to God's will? No
d) What should they have done in this situation? They should have waited since the testing of their Faith produces patience pursuant to James 1:1-6

There was a time span of approximately 26 years between the Promise (Genesis 12:2) and the birth of Isaac, which began the fulfillment of the Promise. God fulfills His promises in His own time. Only God knows the best timing for these things, so we must be patient.

Abraham and Sarah tried to rush God's promise and fulfill it on their own. The result was heartache and seemingly permanent enmity between the descendants of the two half-brothers. God knew this would happen and that it would complicate matters, but in His own purposes it was better this way than to allow Isaac to be born sooner. God can work around our lack of faith, but it is easier on everyone if we trust Him rather than our own efforts.

4. Absalom is another good example of a person who believed the "My Way" lie.

2 Samuel 15:1-12

Absalom's Treason

15 After this it happened that Absalom provided himself with chariots and horses, and fifty men to run before him. ² Now Absalom would rise early and stand beside the way to the gate. So it was, whenever anyone who had a lawsuit came to the king for a decision, that Absalom would call to him and say, "What city are you from?" And he would say, "Your servant is from such and such a tribe of Israel." ³ Then Absalom would say to him, "Look, your case is good and right; but there is no deputy of the king to hear you." ⁴ Moreover Absalom would say, "Oh, that I were made judge in the land, and everyone who has any suit or cause would come to me; then I would give him justice." ⁵ And so it was, whenever anyone came near to bow down to him, that he would put out his hand and take him and kiss him. ⁶ In this manner Absalom acted toward all Israel who came to the king for judgment. So, Absalom stole the hearts of the men of Israel. ⁷ Now it came to pass after [d]forty years that Absalom said to the king, "Please, let me go to Hebron and pay the vow which I made to the LORD. ⁸ For your servant took a vow while I dwelt at Geshur in Syria, saying, 'If the LORD indeed brings me back to Jerusalem, then I will serve the LORD.'"

⁹ And the king said to him, "Go in peace." So, he arose and went to Hebron. ¹⁰ Then Absalom sent spies throughout all the tribes of Israel, saying, "As soon as you hear the sound of the trumpet, then you shall say, 'Absalom reigns in Hebron!'" ¹¹ And with Absalom went two hundred men invited from Jerusalem, and

they went along innocently and did not know anything. [12] Then Absalom sent for Ahithophel the Gilonite, David's counselor, from his city—from Giloh—while he offered sacrifices. And the conspiracy grew strong, for the people with Absalom continually increased in number.

a) What did Absalom do to promote himself?
i) vs. 1: Absalom provided himself with chariots and horses, and fifty men to run before him.

Chariots and horses were a sign of pride (Deuteronomy 17:16, 20). I find it interesting that Solomon sought to surpass all other earthly monarchs in magnificence in exactly the same way. He had 1,400 chariots and 12,000 horsemen in his defense cities and at Jerusalem (1 Kings 10:26-29). Since there were 2 horses for each chariot, this would mean he had 2,800 horses for the chariots. If you add one horse for each horseman, there were a total of 14,800 horses which Solomon introduced into the army of Israel in his day.

ii) vs. 2-5: Now Absalom would rise early and stand beside the way to the gate. So it was, whenever anyone who had a lawsuit came to the king for a decision, that Absalom would call to him and say, "What city are you from?" And he would say, "Your servant is from such and such a tribe of Israel." 3 Then Absalom would say to him, "Look, your case is good and right; but there is no deputy of the king to hear you." 4 Moreover Absalom would say, "Oh, that I were made judge in the land, and everyone who has any suit or cause would come to me; then I would give him justice." 5 And so it was, whenever anyone came near to bow down to him, that he would put out his hand and take him and kiss him.

iii) vs. 6: In this manner Absalom acted toward all Israel who came to the king for judgment. So, Absalom stole the hearts of the men of Israel.

How sad! Absalom was one of the greatest thieves in history. He stole the hearts of the men of Israel by lying, conniving, deceiving, flattering, and playing the part of a hypocrite. The gullibility of men is no better illustrated than in these verses. At one time, when these same people were in trouble, their hearts were with David who delivered them. The character traits of loyalty, devotion, thankfulness, faithfulness, and human decency fell before the tricks of such a smooth deceiver.

iv) vs. 10: Then Absalom sent spies throughout all the tribes of Israel, saying, "As soon as you hear the sound of the trumpet, then you shall say, 'Absalom reigns in Hebron!'"

The spies told the people to listen to the sound of the trumpet. In those days, trumpets were used as a telegraph service, sounding the news from place to place by trumpeting from one trumpet to the next trumpet. In this way, in just a short time, all of Israel could be notified when Absalom was proclaimed king in Hebron.

b) Now read 2 Samuel 18:1-18 to discover how this young man came to an end.:

i) vs. 9: Then Absalom met the servants of David. Absalom rode on a mule. The mule went under the thick boughs of a great terebinth tree, and his head caught in the terebinth; so, he was left hanging between heaven and earth. And the mule which was under him went on.

Actually, since Absalom was trying to escape, I imagine the mule was running rather than walking. Most writers of the commentaries believe that his long, flowing hair got caught in the tree. Either he wore no helmet, or he had thrown it away as well as his other arms, to hasten his flight. However, it may be that his head got caught and wedged between two limbs of the tree.

In the East, riders did not use saddles as we do, and did not sit firmly on the animals as they rode. Absalom must have let go of the bridle, to release himself from the tree, and the mule kept on running.

ii) vs. 14-15: Then Joab said, "I cannot linger with you." And he took three spears in his hand and thrust them through Absalom's heart, while he was still alive in the midst of the terebinth tree. 15 And ten young men who bore Joab's armor surrounded Absalom, and struck and killed him.

The great pile of stones was heaped over his body in accordance with the custom of dishonoring rebels and great criminals by burying them under great piles of stone (Joshua 7:26; Joshua 8:29). The people of the East would indicate their detestation of the memory of such an infamous person by throwing stones at the place where he was buried. The heap grew higher and higher because of the gradual accumulation of stones which passers-by would add to it.

c) Did Absalom accomplish his goals when he set out to make himself happy by seeking "his way? No

d) Explain your answer.: Absalom was defeated and died.

5. Read Hebrews 10:32-39.:

32 But recall the former days in which, after you were illuminated, you endured a great struggle with sufferings: 33 partly while you were made a spectacle both by reproaches and tribulations, and partly while you became companions of those who were so treated; 34 for you had compassion on me in my chains, and joyfully accepted the plundering of your goods, knowing that you have a better and an enduring possession for yourselves in heaven. 35 Therefore do not cast away your confidence, which has great reward. 36 For you have need of endurance, so that after you have done the will of God, you may receive the promise: 37 "For yet a little while, And He who is coming will come and will not tarry. 38 Now the just shall live by faith; But if anyone draws back, My soul has no pleasure

in him." 39 But we are not of those who draw back to perdition, but of those who believe to the saving of the soul.

a) What difficulties did the Hebrews encounter following their conversions?

i) vs. 33a: partly while you were made a spectacle both by reproaches and tribulations,

ii) vs. 33b: and partly while you became companions of those who were so treated;

They also had faced economic persecution (the plundering of your goods). But the point is … they had faced these things and endured. They could look at how they handled persecution in the past, and be encouraged to keep on standing strong in the future.

b) How did the Hebrews act in the midst of these difficulties, when things were not going "their way?":

i) vs. 34a: for you had compassion on me in my chains,

ii) vs. 34b: and joyfully accepted the plundering of your goods,

iii) vs. 34c: knowing that you have a better and an enduring possession for yourselves in heaven.

They made it through the time of persecution by keeping a heavenly perspective.

c) What two things must accompany faith, if we are to receive God's reward when things are not going our way? (vs. 35-36):

i) vs. 35a: Therefore, do not cast away your confidence,

ii) vs. 36a: For you have need of endurance,

d) What reason is there for being confident? (vs. 36): We will receive what God promised after we have done His will.

Faithfulness during the times when the promise seems to be unfulfilled is the measure of your obedience and spiritual maturity.

6. What advice would you give a person operating under the "My Way" thinking error?

Helping them to understand their secure position in the all-sufficient Christ is possible. "Whoever trusts in his own mind is a fool, but he who walks in wisdom will be delivered." That is about as straight forward look at life as you can get. God's way is to everlasting life. For God so loved the world that He gave His only begotten Son, that whoever believes in Him should not perish but have everlasting life. John 3:16

CHAPTER 4

IT IS NOT MY FAULT

"It's Not My Fault."

The concept of a "theology of excuses" suggests an examination of how individuals sometimes rationalize their actions or behaviors through justifications and excuses, often from a moral or ethical standpoint. Theology plays a significant role in critiquing and addressing this phenomenon. It encourages individuals to take responsibility for their actions and decisions, recognizing that excuses can sometimes be a way to avoid accountability. Theological teachings often emphasize the importance of honesty, integrity, and repentance when one has erred, rather than resorting to excuses.

Moreover, theology can challenge the habit of making excuses by promoting self-reflection and introspection. It encourages individuals to examine their motives, intentions, and the impact of their actions on others. In many religious traditions, the pursuit of moral growth and spiritual development involves acknowledging one's shortcomings and seeking forgiveness, rather than relying on a "theology of excuses" as a means of avoiding consequences. By engaging with theology in this way, individuals can strive for greater authenticity and ethical conduct, fostering personal growth and contributing to the well-being of their communities.

Excuses, excuses, excuses! We live in an excuse-prone society. Criminals are excused from crimes because society supposedly did them an "injustice" or they had an unhappy childhood. High-ranking officials in government are excused from their actions because of their positions. Crooks are excused from paying honest debts due to the lenient bankruptcy laws.

And it's not just criminals. We all have a tendency to give a reason for every bad thing that happens. It's as though we need to defend ourselves or try to paint ourselves in a positive light for every scenario. We seem to come pre-programmed with a need to avoid blame, and at times – we will even throw someone else "under the bus" to avoid getting into trouble.

Unfortunately, that attitude is not only used by the world, it is becoming more prevalent among Christians. For example, many will excuse their disobedience in the matter of tithing by saying they just can't afford it. Others excuse their failure to read their Bibles and pray by saying they just don't have time.

Since the very first man and woman, it has always been convenient and guilt-relieving to blame someone else for our actions or circumstances. When cornered by God for breaking the commandment God had given Adam, Adam's excuse was that Eve gave the forbidden fruit to him, so he ate it (Genesis 3:12). Eve's justification for committing the first sin was, "... The serpent beguiled me, and I did eat" (Genesis 3:13). Too often, the way out of avoiding guilt for criminals as well as ourselves is saying it's not our fault, and putting the blame on someone else.

As we read what the Bible teaches us about this blame game problem, we will be motivated to quit making excuses for our problems and mistakes (sins), and start serving Him with all of our might. Let's determine to become problem solvers - not excuse makers!

1. Joseph was a young man who was sold into slavery by his own brothers. Here is a great example of a Bible hero who could have played the "blame game," and said that everything bad that happened in his life was his brothers' fault.

Read Genesis 45:1-15 to see how Joseph responded when he finally met up with his brothers again.:

Genesis 45:1-15

Joseph Revealed to His Brothers

45 Then Joseph could not restrain himself before all those who stood by him, and he cried out, "Make everyone go out from me!" So, no one stood with him while Joseph made himself known to his brothers. 2 And he wept aloud, and the Egyptians and the house of Pharaoh heard it. 3 Then Joseph said to his brothers, "I am Joseph; does my father still live?" But his brothers could not answer him, for they were dismayed in his presence. 4 And Joseph said to his brothers, "Please come near to me." So, they came near. Then he said: "I am Joseph your brother, whom you sold into Egypt. 5 But now, do not therefore be grieved or angry with yourselves because you sold me here; for God sent me before you to preserve life. 6 For these two years the famine has been in the land, and there are still five years in which there will be neither plowing nor harvesting. 7 And God sent me before you to preserve a posterity for you in the earth, and to save your lives by a great deliverance. 8 So now it was not you who sent me here, but God; and He has made me a father to Pharaoh, and lord of all his house, and a ruler throughout all the land of Egypt. 9 "Hurry and go up to my father, and say to him, 'Thus says your son Joseph: "God has made me lord of all Egypt; come down to me, do not tarry. 10 You shall dwell in the land of Goshen, and you shall be near to me, you and your children, your children's children, your flocks and your herds, and all that you have. 11 There I will provide for you, lest you and your household, and all that you have, come to poverty; for there are still five years of famine." 12 "And behold, your eyes and the eyes of my brother Benjamin see that it is my mouth that speaks to you. 13 So you shall tell my father of all my glory in Egypt, and of all that you have seen; and you shall hurry and bring my father down here." 14 Then he fell

on his brother Benjamin's neck and wept, and Benjamin wept on his neck. 15 Moreover he kissed all his brothers and wept over them, and after that his brothers talked with him.

a) Did Joseph find it easy to admit his identity to his brothers? (vs. 1-3):

No

b) How did Joseph's brothers respond to the news? (vs. 3): But his brothers could not answer him, for they were dismayed in his presence.

Because of the punishment they anticipated, the great emotion of Joseph, his manner of revelation, and the total shock of learning Joseph was not only alive but right in front of them, the brothers were dismayed. The ancient Hebrew word for dismayed (bahal) actually means, amazed or frightened or even terrified.

Their dismay was a shadow of what will happen when the Jewish people see Jesus for who He is again: And I will pour on the house of David and on the inhabitants of Jerusalem the Spirit of grace and supplication; then they will look on Me whom they pierced. Yes, they will mourn for Him as one mourns for his only son, and grieve for Him as one grieves for a firstborn. (Zechariah 12:10)

c) Did Joseph spend time accusing and blaming his brothers for what had occurred, or did he retaliate for the unfairness he experienced? (vs. 5):

Joseph forgave them and comforted them. Exhibit: But now, do not therefore be grieved or angry with yourselves because you sold me here; for God sent me before you to preserve life.

Joseph didn't diminish what the brothers had done when they sold him into slavery in Egypt. But he saw that God's purpose in it all was greater than the evil of the brothers. Joseph had been the victim of a malicious plan, but God turned it around for His glory. None of it was for a loss.

d) What guidance does Joseph provide for responding when we believe something bad that happened to us was someone else's fault? (vs. 9-15): 9

"Hurry and go up to my father, and say to him, 'Thus says your son Joseph: "God has made me lord of all Egypt; come down to me, do not [a]tarry. 10 You shall dwell in the land of Goshen, and you shall be near to me, you and your children, your children's children, your flocks and your herds, and all that you have. 11 There I will provide for you, lest you and your household, and all that you have, come to poverty; for there are still five years of famine."

2. Read Genesis 39. Again, Joseph experienced unfair treatment when he was unjustly accused by Potiphar's wife. He ended up in Potiphar's prison, and it would have been quite true to say it was somebody else's fault that he landed in jail. However, instead of whining and complaining, Joseph used this time to serve Potiphar within the prison system and to serve God:

a) What was the secret of Joseph's success? (vs. 2-3): 2 The Lord was with Joseph, and he was a successful man; and he was in the house of his master the Egyptian. 3 And his master saw that the Lord was with him and that the Lord made all he did to prosper in his hand.

God blessed all Joseph did, as is always the case when God is "with" someone. Following are a few other examples of God being "with" men.

1. Ishmael (Genesis 21:20)
2. Abraham (Genesis 21:22)
3. Jacob (Genesis 28:15)
4. Joseph (Genesis 39:2)
5. Moses (Joshua 1:5)
6. Joshua (Joshua 1:5, 9)
7. Samuel (1 Samuel 3:19)

b) How did Joseph's success affect Potiphar's situation? (vs. 4-5):

4 So Joseph found favor in his sight, and served him. Then he made him overseer of his house, and all that he had he put under his authority. 5 So it was, from the time that he had made him overseer of his house and all that he had, that the Lord blessed the Egyptian's house for Joseph's sake; and the blessing of the Lord was on all that he had in the house and in the field.

c) What made Joseph's responsibilities difficult? (vs. 6-7): 6 Thus he left all that he had in Joseph's hand, and he did not know what he had except for the bread which he ate.

The beauty of Joseph was celebrated all over the East. Persian poets and the 12th chapter of the Koran speak of his beauty as perfect. Old Eastern traditions say that Potiphar's wife was at first the most virtuous of women, but when she saw him, she was so affected that she lost all self-control (self-discipline), and became a slave to her passion for him. Another interesting story (not in the Bible) is that on one occasion she supposedly made a dinner and invited 40 of the most beautiful women of Egypt. When they saw Joseph, they were so moved with admiration that they exclaimed with one accord that he must be an angel.

d) Was this an isolated event? (vs. 10-12): Yes - hmmmm, I wonder.

The story of Joseph is a good example of a man living a disciplined life. Too many of us think we have the strength to face down temptations from the middle of the situation. When Joseph ran from Potiphar's wife, Joseph showed us when it is good to make a stand, and when it is better to remove ourselves from people who lack self-discipline.

e) How did going to prison affect God's blessing on Joseph? (vs. 21-23):

21 But the Lord was with Joseph and showed him mercy, and He gave him favor in the sight of the keeper of the prison. 22 And the keeper of the prison committed to Joseph's hand all the prisoners who were in the prison; whatever they did there, it was his doing. 23 The keeper of the prison did not look into anything that was under Joseph's authority, because the Lord was with him; and whatever he did, the Lord made it prosper.

3. Now read Judges 11. Jephthah had a difficult childhood. His mother was a harlot or, by the terms of today, a prostitute. As if that wasn't enough, he was disowned and disinherited by his family because of it. But Jephthah didn't sit around complaining, feeling sorry for himself, and blaming others for his bad luck. Instead, Jephthah gathered a band of men, and operated somewhat like David and his men did during the period described in 1 Samuel 25:4-8, protecting cities and settlements from marauders and receiving pay from those whom they helped.:

a) When Ammon made war against Israel, what did the elders of Gilead ask Jephthah to do? (vs. 5-8): hey said to Jephthah, "Come and be our commander, that we may fight against the people of Ammon."

The nation of Ammon, the Ammonites, lived to the south of Israel. They were a semi-nomadic group of people who were descendants of Abraham's nephew Lot. Because of the crisis of the Ammonites, the leaders of Gilead were desperate for an able leader, and they turned to Jephthah. They were willing to give him the authority as head over Gilead.

b) What did Jephthah ask for in return? (vs. 9-11): Jephthah said to the elders of Gilead, "If you take me back home to fight against the people of Ammon, and the Lord delivers them to me, shall I be your head?"

Yes. Jephthah was only willing to assume leadership in the crisis if he could also remain a leader after the crisis. He didn't want to be rejected again as a worthless man.

c) Was Jephthah successful? (vs. 32): Yes

d) What are we told about Jephthah in Hebrews 11:32-34?

Through faith subdued kingdoms, worked righteousness, obtained promises, stopped the mouths of lions, 34 quenched the violence of fire, escaped the edge of the sword, out of weakness were made strong, became valiant in battle, turned to fight the armies of the aliens.

Each one of the men mentioned in these verses were men of faith, yet each one also had notable areas of failure in their life. Jephthah was used of God to defeat the Ammonites, but he made a foolish vow and then stubbornly kept it (Judges 11:30-40).

Still, Hebrews 11 commends their faith and lists them in the "Hall of Faith." This shows that even though we all make mistakes, by our faith in Jesus alone for salvation we will still make it into God's "Hall of Faith."

4. One Christian from a less than desirable background used it to excuse his sinful behavior. Another Christian from a nearly identical background used his situation growing up as a motivation to serve God and minister to others. How do you explain the difference?

Some will use excuses and excuses to support their behavior and why they are, in contrast, the other will use said situation to change his life just like Jephthah who had a difficult childhood but did not remain there and change his life and depended on the Lord.

5. What advice would you give a person operating under the "Not My Fault" thinking error?

To quit making excuses for our problems and mistakes (sins), and start serving Him with all of our might. Let's determine to become problem solvers - not excuse makers!

In this last example, Jephthah had a difficult childhood. He could have said "It's not my fault," because his mother was a prostitute and he was disowned and disinherited by his family because of it. But he didn't sit around complaining and feeling sorry for himself. The Bible records that "The Spirit of the Lord came upon Jephthah" and God greatly used him.

We can all rise above our circumstances and be greatly used by God as well.

CHAPTER 5

THAT WASN'T
FAIR

"That Wasn't Fair."

Fairness is encouraged in the classroom, and at home, and has fostered the belief in some people that life should be fair all the time. The criminal mind tends to harbor a grudge for a past injustice, real or perceived, for years – and at the right moment, take steps to "even the score." Vengeful behavior may also be targeted at people who seem to have gotten more than they deserve. People with this mindset will believe they put in equal or more effort, and should have gotten at least the same if not more. They keep score, and may steal or destroy the property of others to even things up.

Others become angered, and may even turn to violence, when they perceive a person didn't get what they deserve or got less than they deserve, perhaps, in the courtroom. One of their family members may have been the victim of a crime, and their friends encouraged them to be patient and let the law handle it. Then, to their dismay, the charges were dropped due to a technicality, or the perpetrator got off with a simple "slap on the wrist."

A person with the "life should be fair" mindset may decide to take the law into their own hands, rather than waiting on God to take care of the injustice. They may execute what they consider to be a fair punishment themselves, or find/hire someone else to do it. This isn't a new idea. In America, this practice started back during the time of the "Old Wild West", when the nearest sheriff may have been a day's ride away. Lynching parties were common for horse thieves. And hired guns were a commodity for the filthy rich. Today there are still vigilantes, terrorists, and mercenaries who will "take care of business" for a price.

The spiritual issue with always wanting life to be fair is that it tempts us to let anger, resentment, and bitterness take up residence in our heart. Anger itself isn't a sin, but venting our anger can be destructive. We need to learn to wait on God, and seek His perspective on the situation.

1. When someone is operating under this thinking error, vengeful behavior may be targeted at ….:

a): people who seem to have gotten more than they deserve.

b): People with this mindset will believe they put in equal or more effort, and should have gotten at least the same if not more.

But God, who is eminently fair, gives different gifts to everyone: "Shall what is formed say to the one who formed it, 'Why did you make me like this?'" (Romans 9:20). Our responsibility is to use the gifts God has given and "be content with what [we] have" (Hebrews 13:5).

c): They keep score, and may steal or destroy the property of others to even things up.

At times we've all been tempted to cry out, "Lord, it's just not fair! Why do You allow the wicked to get away with things, while believers suffer even though they didn't even do anything wrong? It's just not fair!"

2. The theological truth about the thinking error called "The Fallacy of Fairness" is found in Ecclesiastes 8:14. It says that there are 2 seemingly unjust things in life:

Ecclesiastes 8:14

New King James Version [14] There is a vanity which occurs on earth, that there are just men to whom it happens according to the work of the wicked; again, there are wicked men to whom it happens according to the work of the righteous. I said that this also is vanity.

a): that there are just men to whom it happens according to the work of the wicked;

b): there are wicked men to whom it happens according to the work of the righteous.

How many of us, as children, were admonished with the self-evident truth that "life's not fair"? It's a hard lesson, but it's one we all learned, usually before we got out of kindergarten.

3. Ecclesiastes 9:11 says, "I also saw other things in this life that were not fair. The fastest runner does not always win the race; the strongest soldier does not always win the battle; wise people don't always get the food; smart people don't always get the wealth; educated people don't always get the praise they deserve. When the time comes, bad things can happen to anyone" (ERV). What does this verse say about whether life is fair or not?

As adults, we are surrounded by evidence that life is not fair. Driving our 10 to 20-year-old cars, we drive past multi-million-dollar homes with pristine lawns and ridiculously expensive sports cars parked in the driveway. We see people throwing money around as if it were confetti, while we struggle to pay the electric bill and keep food on the table. We see those who flaunt the law yet get off scot-free, and we see others who are innocent yet are punished unjustly.

4. Read John 10:10.:

^{10} The thief does not come except to steal, and to kill, and to destroy. I have come that they may have life, and that they may have it more abundantly.

a) What does the thief come to do? to steal, and to kill, and to destroy.

The "thief" here is the shepherd who steals someone else's sheep. He will kill the sheep and destroy the flock. The thief in this context is the Pharisee. The Pharisees wanted to take advantage of the flock.

b) Who is the thief? Satan

Justice and fairness are closely related terms that are often today used interchangeably.

c) When a person kills, steals, or destroys to even the score, whose work are they doing? Satan work

5. In the story of Cain and Abel, we find first story recorded in the Bible where a person who thought, "That wasn't fair," acted on his feelings. Read Genesis 4.:

a) Why did Cain and Abel bring sacrifices to God? (Numbers 18:12, 17; Leviticus 3:16; Revelations 13:8): It was sacrifice for atonement for sin

I believe Cain and Abel were doing this because God had revealed to them that this was the right thing to do – in thanksgiving and to atone for their sins. But how were Cain and Abel supposed to know what would be an acceptable sacrifice? The answer is that God must have instructed them. It is clear that the offering was to be a substitutionary atonement, because we read in Hebrews 11:4, "By faith Abel offered God a better sacrifice than Cain did."

b) Why did Cain kill Abel? Because his sacrifice was rejected Correct. We do not know how God expressed His rejection, but it was evident to both of them.

c) Why did God prefer the sacrifice of Abel?

It was animal sacrifice. Animal sacrifice is acceptable as an atonement for sin, not fruits. Also, the attitude of their hearts by what they offer is different. Abel gave the first and the best, while Cain simply gave an offering. Abel displayed his faith and dependence on God's providence, and Cain did not.

Cain's offering was unacceptable because it was bloodless (see Leviticus 17:11). He was perverting God's prescribed form of worship.

d) How did Abel offer his sacrifice "by faith?" (See Hebrews 9:22 and 11:4): By faith Abel offered to God a more excellent sacrifice than Cain, through which he obtained witness that he was righteous, God testifying of his gifts; and through it he being dead still speaks.

Without shedding of blood there is no remission of sin. This is a foundational principle of God's dealings with men. Modern people think that sin is remitted (forgiven) over time, by our good works, by our decent lives, or when we die. But there is no forgiveness without the shedding of blood, and there is no perfect forgiveness without a perfect sacrifice.

When Jesus died on the cross, He became the substitutionary atonement (took our place) for our sins by shedding His own precious blood, and offered the perfect sacrifice to the Father for the remission of all our sins.

e) How did God punish Cain?
God punished Cain by condemning him to a life of wandering.

6. We already studied in Chapter 4 how Joseph handled himself in unfair situations. Now let's study Moses' reaction to an unfair situation. Read Exodus 2:11-12 and then Acts 7:24-25.:

Exodus 2:11-12

Moses Flees to Midian

[11] Now it came to pass in those days, when Moses was grown, that he went out to his brethren and looked at their burdens. And he saw an Egyptian beating a Hebrew, one of his brethren. [12] So he looked this way and that way, and when he saw no one, he killed the Egyptian and hid him in the sand.

Acts 7:24-25

[24] And seeing one of them suffer wrong, he defended and avenged him who was oppressed, and struck down the Egyptian. [25] For he supposed that his brethren would have understood that God would deliver them by his hand, but they did not understand.

a) What did Moses observe that was unfair?
He saw an Egyptian beating a Hebrew, one of his brethren.
Moses had a heart filled with sympathy toward his own people. He just couldn't stand by while one of his fellow Israelites endured an unfair beating.

b) How did Moses handle the situation?
He killed the Egyptian and hid him in the sand.

Acts 7:23 says this happened when Moses was forty years old. Up until then, he was trained and groomed to become the next Pharaoh of Egypt (according to Josephus), all the while aware of his true origins because of his mother. By faith, Moses deliberately decided to identify with the people of Israel rather than his Egyptian prestige and opportunity.

c) Did Moses sin? Moses committed two sins, first because he committed murder and also because he did not wait on God to handle things.

And we know his conscience bothered him, because the Scripture says "he looked this way and that," and then he "hid him in the sand." These are the actions of a person who knows he did something wrong.

7. Matthew 20:1-16 demonstrates "The Fallacy of Fairness" mindset perfectly.:

a) What did the landlord promise to pay the first group he hired? (vs. 2): a denarius a day

The word is uniformly translated "penny" in the King James Version and "shilling" in the American Standard Revised Version, except in Matthew 22:19; Mark 12:15 and Luke 20:24, where the Latin word is used, since in these passages it refers to the coin in which tribute was paid to the Roman government. It took 25 denarius to equal the aureus, the standard gold coin of the empire in the time of Augustus. This gold coin was equal in value to about $5.00 in today's currency, so each denarius would be worth about 20 cents.

A denarius was the common worker's wage for a day's labor. Vineyard labor was seasonal and depended on the size of the harvest. These laborers were undoubtedly very happy to have someone hire them. In other places and other times, these workers may not have been able to find the work they needed to feed their families.

b) What did he promise to pay those whom he hired later? (vs.4-5): whatever is right I will give you.

He did not promise them a full day's wage, but he did promise to pay them what was right. It was common to recruit workers in city squares and shopping districts. These workers may have been traveling from district to district looking for work. If they had been in the same place all day, either the landowner had not seen them before, or he had found that he needed more laborers as the day went on.

c) How much did he pay the men who had worked only one hour? (vs. 9): He received a denarius.
The steward had been made the payroll clerk that day, but he could only pay out what the landowner told him.

d) How much did those who had worked all day receive? (vs. 10): each received a denarius.

Imagine their joy when those who had worked for a single hour were paid a full day's wages.

e) Were all the workers happy with their pay?

Did this seem fair to them? they complained against the landowner,

But those at the end of the pay line saw that those who had worked only an hour had received a full day's wage. Their expectations went up, thinking that the landowner would pay them in proportion to the amount of labor they had put in. Perhaps they reasoned that if a person who worked one hour received a denarius then those who worked eleven hours should receive eleven denarii.

However, their expectations were not met. Instead, they received a denarius just as they had been promised. In their own minds, they felt it was unfair that those who had worked so little had received the same wage as those who had worked longer and under harsher conditions.

We are not told how the full-time workers found out about the wages of the part-timers. However, if they had not known, then they would have been happy with the wages they received. Therefore, the "unfairness" was only in their minds and was based on unfounded expectations.

f) Was the landowner unfair in the way he treated the all-day workers? (vs. 12-15): No he was not. They did agree for denarius a day.

It was the landowner's right to pay whatever he wanted to whomever he wanted for the labor that they did. The landowner exceeded the expectations of those who worked less, and it was his prerogative to do so. The long-hour labors became jealous and wanted more than they were entitled to. Their complaint had no basis because the landowner paid them exactly what they had agreed to.

Jesus promised that all people who believe in Him will have eternal life with Him and share in God's unending goodness and love. What more could we ask for?

Some people become Christians at a very young age. Others may not become Christians until they are near death. In each case, the wage is the same. Some live as Christians under oppression and persecution -- even to the point of being executed for their faith. Others live in relative comfort with little conflict. Yet, the wage will be the same.

However, there will be no place for jealousy in heaven. God has already agreed to "pay" us far beyond what we deserve. All of us will be overjoyed at the rich generosity of God and humbled by the recognition of his or her own unworthiness.

8. This parable leads to a question for all of us today. How should a Christian respond when treated unfairly, especially on the job? Is it wrong to defend yourself or to stand up for your rights? That is the question Peter addresses in 1 Peter 2:18-24.:

1 Peter 2:18-24

Submission to Masters

18 Servants, be submissive to your masters with all fear, not only to the good and gentle, but also to the harsh. 19 For this is commendable, if because of conscience toward God one endures grief, suffering wrongfully. 20 For what credit is it if, when you are beaten for your faults, you take it patiently? But when you do good and suffer, if you take it patiently, this is commendable before God. 21 For to this you were called, because Christ also suffered for [a]us, leaving [b]us an example, that you should follow His steps: 22 "Who committed no sin, Nor was deceit found in His mouth"; 23 who, when He was reviled, did not revile in return; when He suffered, He did not threaten, but committed Himself to Him who judges righteously; 24 who Himself bore our sins in His own body on the tree, that we, having died to sins, might live for righteousness—by whose [c]stripes you were healed.

a) To whom are employees to be subject? Submission to Masters

b) How are they to respond to both good and bad bosses? Servants, be submissive to your masters with all fear, not only to the good and gentle, but also to the harsh.

9. Summary of what you learn about suffering and/or being treated unfairly in 1 Peter 2:19-24.:

a) How is a believer to respond to suffering? For this is commendable, if because of conscience toward God one endures grief, suffering wrongfully.

b) How should you respond when you are treated unfairly? But when you do good and suffer, if you take it patiently, this is commendable before God.

c) How does God view a proper response to suffering? We should follow Christ who "Who committed no sin, Nor was deceit found in His mouth"; but suffered.

The command to submit to masters isn't just to those who work for masters that are good and gentle, but also to those who are harsh. If we must endure hardship because of our Christian standards, it is then commendable before God.

d) How did Jesus respond when He was punished unfairly for our sins? He did not threaten, but committed Himself to Him who judges righteously;

10. What advice would you give a person operating under the "That Wasn't Fair" thinking error?

CHAPTER 6

WHATEVER

"Whatever!"

What do people mean when they answer with … "whatever"? Anyone who hears you say it knows you don't give a hoot about any decision that needs to be made. The problem is not the word itself. The problem is that any time the word is used it means you are not making a choice — and life is all about small choices. Seemingly small decisions are a part of each and every day, and it is easy to ignore them. When the word "whatever" is used as a reply, you are simply not making a decision.

What is a person really thinking when he/she uses the "whatever" word?

- I don't care.
- You make the decision for me; I will blame you later.
- If I knew the answer, I would tell you. So, leave me alone.
- I am not listening.
- Of all the options presented, none are good, but I'll make you suffer anyway.
- I am really angry and will hold you responsible for any decision you make for me.
- I don't have an opinion so I will fill the air with this useless word.
- I am resigned to being a victim.

The "whatever" word is also sometimes used as a "fronting" tactic by criminals. In this case, people use the word to imply they don't care one way or the other, but they're actually manipulating that person. They're saying they'll go along with you on this, but then you're going to owe them big time. They're playing a role,

49

doing something they don't really want to do in order to bank a favor, to get something back later in return.

From another viewpoint, the "whatever" word takes away responsibility for an action. It wasn't their idea, it wasn't their decision, they're just going along for the ride. If it all goes south and the law gets involved - it wasn't their fault.

"Whatever" doesn't work with God. We don't get an opportunity for "fronting" with Him, and we won't be able to shirk responsibility when we get caught. He alone makes the rules and determines truth. He requires a definite decision from us one way or the other, and there are only two options. Deuteronomy 30:19 says, "I call heaven and earth to record this day against you, that I have set before you life and death, blessing and cursing: therefore, choose life that both thou and thy seed may live."

1. Why won't the "whatever" answer work with God?

God requires a definite decision from us one way or the other, and there are only two options. Exhibited in Deuteronomy 30:19 "I call heaven and earth to record this day against you, that I have set before you, life and death, blessing and cursing: therefore, choose life that both thou and thy seed may live."

I think the best comeback for "whatever" is silence - whether it was said to those around us or directly to God. Usually the word "whatever" is said with a tone, an edge, with sneakiness and resentment. It is a word that indicates the listener is bored, disinterested, or doesn't care what you think. The basic problem here is usually a bad attitude.

2. When faced with a decision, your choices aren't just selecting one option or another. The third dimension of decision-making is saying "whatever" and refusing to select either one – which is actually making a decision.: True

3. According to Deuteronomy 30:19, what are our two choices?

[19] I call heaven and earth as witnesses today against you, that I have set before you, life and death, blessing and cursing; therefore, choose life, that both you and your descendants may live;

a): life and death

b): blessing and cursing

Although the choice belonged to Israel, God cared about what they chose. When Moses pled with Israel, crying out choose life, we know he reflected the heart of God toward Israel.

4. The phrase "I call heaven and earth to record against you" means ... (vs. 19): I ask heaven and earth to be witnesses.

5. What is the five-fold benefit of making the right choices? (Deuteronomy 30:19-20):

[19] I call heaven and earth as witnesses today against you, that I have set before you, life and death, blessing and cursing; therefore choose life, that both you and your descendants may live; [20] that you may love the LORD your God, that you may obey His voice, and that you may cling to Him, for He is your life and the length of your days; and that you may dwell in the land which the LORD swore to your fathers, to Abraham, Isaac, and Jacob, to give them."

a) vs. 19e: that both you and your descendants may live;

b) vs. 20a: that you may love the Lord your God,

c) vs. 20b: that you may obey His voice

To love and trust God means to obey His voice, just like a child who really loves and trusts his father will obey him. It means to cling to Him, for if we really love and trust Him, we will be attached to Him. If we love and trust Him, He won't a distant part of our lives. He will be our everything.

d)   vs.   20c: and   that   you   may   cling   to   Him,

e) vs. 20e: for He is your life and the length of your days;

6. Joshua gives us a very good example of making good choices. Read Joshua 24:14-18. What four things did Joshua tell people they must do, in order to serve the Lord in sincerity and in truth?

Joshua 24:14-18

14 "Now therefore, fear the LORD, serve Him in sincerity and in truth, and put away the gods which your fathers served on the other side of the River and in Egypt. Serve the LORD! 15 And if it seems evil to you to serve the LORD, choose for yourselves this day whom you will serve, whether the gods which your fathers served that were on the other side of the River, or the gods of the Amorites, in whose land you dwell. But as for me and my house, we will serve the LORD." 16 So the people answered and said: "Far be it from us that we should forsake the LORD to serve other gods; 17 for the LORD our God is He who brought us and our fathers up out of the land of Egypt, from the house of bondage, who did those great signs in our sight, and preserved us in all the way that we went and among all the people through whom we passed. 18 And the LORD drove out from before us all the people, including the Amorites who dwelt in the land. We also will serve the LORD, for He is our God."

This passage was Joshua's farewell speech to the Israelites. The people still did not fully possess the Promised Land. There would be more battles to fight. Losing a leader like Joshua probably caused the people to be anxious. But Joshua reminded them of God's faithfulness and challenged them to serve God.

a)   vs. 14a: Now therefore, fear the Lord,

b) vs. 14b: serve Him in sincerity and in truth,

Sincerity is the exact opposite of the hypocrisy we so often see today, even among believers.

b) vs. 14c: and put away the gods which your fathers served on the other side of the river and in Egypt.

a) God had demonstrated His divine power and care to Israel - from the day they left Egypt until this day.

b) He had proven that He was the only God and that He was worthy of all worship.

c) Joshua encouraged the people to look at the evidence and then destroy the idols from among themselves, lest they suffer the consequences from God, who would not tolerate and substitutes for Him.

d) vs. 14d: Serve the Lord

7. a) When Joshua gave them two choices, did the people answer with "whatever"?

The Israelites had real options to choose from, and Joshua wanted them to commit to the only option that would really benefit them. Abraham had left the gods of his father to serve the only living God. God had demonstrated before Israel's eyes that the so-called gods of the Egyptians and Canaanites were no match for Him. God visibly demonstrated His power and love to the Israelites, so the best choice was obvious to them.

But the choice to serve God or not is always immediate. When people hear and see what God has done, they decide instantly whether to believe it or not. But delaying the choice to serve is usually a decision not to follow God until something "more convincing" happens. However, if a person is to serve God, it is better for him to choose to do so as soon as he can. One might fool himself into thinking he can serve God later in life, but he may not have the time or ability to choose God on his deathbed. Once a person has dies, he can no longer choose to serve God. Therefore, it is imperative for those reading to "choose this day" whether to serve God or turn away.

c)   If not, how did they answer? We also will serve the Lord, for He is our God."

8. What reasons did the people give for making that choice? (vs. 17-18):

a): for the Lord our God is He who brought us and our fathers up out of the land of Egypt, from the house of bondage,

b): who did those great signs in our sight, and preserved us in all the way that we went and among all the people through whom we passed.

c): And the Lord drove out from before us all the people, including the Amorites who dwelt in the land. We also will serve the Lord, for He is our God."

Israel promised to serve God alone based on the works He had done in their lifetimes. He had certainly earned their respect, and the people were sincerely grateful.

9. Now there is actually an instance in scripture where the Apostle Paul in effect said, "Whatever," and it's a good example of a person being totally submitted to God's will. Read Philippians 1:20-25.:

Philippians 1:20-25

20 according to my earnest expectation and hope that in nothing I shall be ashamed, but with all boldness, as always, so now also Christ will be magnified in my body, whether by life or by death. 21 For to me, to live is Christ, and to die is gain. 22 But if I live on in the flesh, this will mean fruit from my labor; yet what I shall choose I cannot tell. 23 For I am hard-pressed between the two, having a desire to depart and be with Christ, which is far better. 24 Nevertheless to remain in the flesh is more needful for you. 25 And being confident of this, I know that I shall remain and continue with you all for your progress and joy of faith,

a) What were the two possibilities that might occur in Paul's life at that time?

i): For to me, to live is Christ,

ii): and to die is gain.

b) Paul knew that the Lord was in control of all events including his imprisonment, so either way he ...: remain and continue with you all for your progress and joy of faith,

c) Although we might see death as a negative, Paul believed his death would be a positive in two ways.:

i) His death for the cause of Christ would glorify Christ

ii) If he died, he knew he would to be in the immediate presence of the Lord

These were words of faith. Though he was in prison and awaiting trial before Caesar, Paul had the confidence that he was in the center of God's will. He knew God was not punishing him through the adversity he experienced at the time. Paul mightily trusted God here, and Paul first trusted God that in nothing I shall be ashamed. He believed that God would not cause him to be ashamed or that God would not turn against him in the matter.

10. How would you counsel a person who habitually uses the "Whatever" response?

Please inform the individual that the word he/she used is a neutral answer and not a choice between two options. Encourage the person to decide and be responsible for his/her life.

CHAPTER 7

I CAN'T

"I Can't."

Do you ever catch yourself using the "I can't…" excuse when things aren't lining up the way you wanted? Have you ever refused to take responsibility for the events or circumstances of your life? Or have you ever tried to explain why you didn't, couldn't, or simply wouldn't do something?

With the "I can't" mentality, people present themselves as being helpless, unable to meet expectations and in need of others' help. This thinking error is very similar to victim stance. Using helplessness as an excuse, this person will talk about how, "I can't get a job", "I can't find a place to live", or "I can't overcome my disabilities." This is another way of exercising control over others. But if we confront the person for using the "I can't" excuse, they will accuse us of being discriminatory or uncaring.

With this excuse, a person will often try to avoid doing what is required or expected. For example, a person might say, "I couldn't possibly keep all those rules. There's too many and I can't keep them all straight in my head." The person who says "I can't," often really means "I won't," and this excuse could lead to the loss of a job or even the loss of freedom.

In other situations, the person using the "I can't" excuse is afraid of failing or being embarrassed. Fear can trap people in their comfort zone and leave them locked up while creating an illusion of security. Using this excuse to defend their lack of action, they will cripple their ability to move forward. Unable to advance through lawful channels, they may turn to crime to get what they want.

A few of our heroes in Bible times tried to get out of their assignments from the Lord by using the "I can't" or "I'm not able" excuse. That rationale didn't fly with God then, and it still doesn't work with Him today.

1. Read Judges 6:11-16.:

Judges 6:11-16

Gideon

11 Now the Angel of the LORD came and sat under the terebinth tree which was in Ophrah, which belonged to Joash the Abiezrite, while his son Gideon threshed wheat in the winepress, in order to hide it from the Midianites. 12 And the Angel of the LORD appeared to him, and said to him, "The LORD is with you, you mighty man of valor!" 13 Gideon said to Him, "O [a]my lord, if the LORD is with us, why then has all this happened to us? And where are all His miracles which our fathers told us about, saying, 'Did not the LORD bring us up from Egypt?' But now the LORD has forsaken us and delivered us into the hands of the Midianites." 14 Then the LORD turned to him and said, "Go in this might of yours, and you shall save Israel from the hand of the Midianites. Have I not sent you?" 15 So he said to Him, "O [b]my Lord, how can I save Israel? Indeed, my clan is the weakest in Manasseh, and I am the least in my father's house." 16 And the LORD said to him, "Surely I will be with you, and you shall defeat the Midianites as one man."

a) What assignment did the Lord give to Gideon? Go in this might of yours, and you shall save Israel from the hand of the Midianites.

We don't see the evidence that Gideon had any "might" or strength to go in. Yet the Angel of the Lord wasn't making fun of Gideon when he told him, "Go in this might of yours." Gideon had the might of the weak, and the Apostle Paul reminds us that God's strength is perfected in weakness (2 Corinthians 12:9).

b) What excuses did Gideon offer? (vs. 15)

i): So, he said to Him, "O my Lord, how can I save Israel?

ii): Indeed, my clan is the weakest in Manasseh, and I am the least in my father's house."

Gideon couldn't imagine himself as someone who could possibly do great things for God. He thought of himself as insignificant. He came from the smallest clan in his tribe, and he saw himself as the least in his own family.

c) How did the Lord respond to Gideon's excuses? (vs. 16): And the Lord said to him, "Surely I will be with you, and you shall defeat the Midianites as one man."

God's assurance to Gideon was not to build up his self-confidence, but to assure him that God was indeed with him. Gideon did not need more self-confidence; he needed more God-confidence.

2. Read Exodus Chapters 3 and 4.:

a) What assignment did the Lord give to Moses? (Exodus 3:10): Come now, therefore, and I will send you to Pharaoh that you may bring My people, the children of Israel, out of Egypt."

God could have brought the people out of Egypt all by Himself, but it is most often God's plan to work with and through people, as we are workers together with Him (2 Corinthians 6:1).

b) What objections did Moses raise to try to get out of the job?

i) Exodus 4:1: hen Moses answered and said, "But suppose they will not believe me or listen to my voice; suppose they say, 'The Lord has not appeared to you.'

It was good that Moses had no confidence in his own ability, but it was bad that he then lacked confidence in God. In Exodus

3:18, God had already promised that the leaders of Israel would listen to Moses. He said, "They will heed your voice." So, when Moses made this protest, he may as well have been saying, "But what if you are wrong, God?"

ii) Exodus 4:10: Then Moses said to the Lord, "O my Lord, I am not eloquent, neither before nor since You have spoken to Your servant; but I am slow of speech and slow of tongue.

But Moses' excuse was not justified. Clearly 40 years before this Moses was not slow of speech and slow of tongue. Acts 7:22 says Moses was learned in all the wisdom of the Egyptians, and was mighty in words and deeds. But for the last 40 years, he had only been talking to sheep. His self-confidence was gone.

c) How did God respond to each of his excuses?

i): So, the Lord said to him, "Who has made man's mouth? Or who makes the mute, the deaf, the seeing, or the blind? Have not I, the Lord?

ii): 12 Now therefore, go, and I will be with your mouth and teach you what you shall say."

Commentaries say that when God brought Aaron to help lead with Moses, it was an expression of His chastening to Moses, not of His approval or giving in to Moses. As it turned out, Aaron was more of a problem to Moses than a help.

Aaron instigated the worship of the golden calf, fashioning the calf himself and building the altar himself (Exodus 32:1-6). Aaron's sons blasphemed God with impure offerings (Leviticus 10:1-7). At one time, Aaron openly led a mutiny against Moses (Numbers 12:1-8).

Aaron was a smooth talker, but Moses might have looked back at when the Lord gave Aaron to Moses as a partner – and wished he had taken on the assignment alone.

d) What if Moses hadn't obeyed? What if Moses had flat out refused? (Thought question - answers will vary.): The Lord would have punished him and lose the prophetic office.

We can't point our fingers at Moses. We all have fears. Too often, though, believers have let them rule over their lives and stop them from stepping out in faith when God has given them an assignment.

The expression "Never let one money stop the show" comes to my mind. I think God would have selected someone else to lead the people out of Egypt and into the Promised Land.

3. Now in Matthew 17, there actually was a situation where the disciples tried to do something and had to admit they had failed.: Matthew 17:15-16

[15] "Lord, have mercy on my son, for he is an epileptic and suffers severely; for he often falls into the fire and often into the water. [16] So I brought him to Your disciples, but they could not cure him."

a) What did the disciples attempt to do? (vs. 15-16): The disciples attempted to cure an epileptic boy

The parallel narrative in Mark 9:14-29 tells us that the boy was made deaf and dumb by this demon.

b) But why did Jesus say they were unable to do it? (vs. 20): "Because of their unbelief;

This failure was actually good for them, because it taught them several lessons.

- They learned it wasn't good to get into a "how to" rut of mechanical ministry. Each situation and need were different.
- It reminded them of the great superiority of Jesus' power and ministry.
- It made them long for the presence of Jesus.
- It taught them to come to Jesus with their problems.

4. The same choice is before us today. God has an assignment for each of us, something we were uniquely created to do. Are we making excuses so we don't have obey?

Are we making excuses so we don't have to do what we know God wants us to do or to go where He wants us to go?

Are we making excuses for why we will not trust Him for success in the assignment?

You may say "I can't", but God says you can. Check out the following verses for God's answer to many of our excuses.:

a) You say, "It's impossible." God says ... (Luke 18:27), "The things which are impossible with men are possible with God."

b) You say, "I'm too tired." God says ... (Matthew 11:28-30): 28 Come to Me, all you who labor and are heavy laden, and I will give you rest. 29 Take My yoke upon you and learn from Me, for I am gentle and lowly in heart, and you will find rest for your souls. 30 For My yoke is easy and My burden is light."

c) You say, "I can't go on." God says ... (2 Corinthians 12:9): 9 And He said to me, "My grace is sufficient for you, for My strength is made perfect in weakness." Therefore, most gladly I will rather boast in my infirmities, that the power of Christ may rest upon me.

d) You say, "I can't figure things out." God says ... (Proverbs 3:5-6): Trust in the Lord with all your heart, and lean not on your own understanding; In all your ways acknowledge Him, And He shall direct your paths.

e) You say, "I can't do it." God says ... (Philippians 4:13): I can do all things through Christ who strengthens me.

f) You say, "I'm not able." God says ... (Corinthians 9:8): And God is able to make all grace abound toward you, that you, always having all sufficiency in all things, may have an abundance for every good work.

g) You say, "I can't because I'm not smart enough." God says ... (James 1:5): If any of you lacks wisdom, let him ask of God, who gives to all liberally and without reproach, and it will be given to him.

Wisdom is the correct use of knowledge. It is the ability to apply the discernment and judgment of God's Word to real life situations. In other words, if we don't know how to apply the Word to our experience, we lack wisdom.

The word used for "ask" here means to request, to plead for, to call for. It implies asking for something with urgency, even to the point of demanding. And God is generous with those who ask from Him. He doesn't give His gifts grudgingly. He doesn't complain about answering our prayers. He delights in doing so, and will give wisdom to those who ask.

5. What advice would you give a person operating under the "I Can't" thinking error?

Please use Philippians 4:13 that I can do all things through Christ who gives us strength. As Jesus said in Matthew 19:26 But Jesus looked at them and said to them, "With men this is impossible, but with God all things are possible."

CHAPTER 8

I DIN'T DO ANYTHING WRONG

"I Didn't Do Anything Wrong."

Everyone has a conscience. Our conscience is a God-given awareness of what is right and what is wrong. In Romans 2:14-15, Paul said that the Gentiles already knew they were sinners because of the unwritten law that was written in their hearts. For believers today, a nudge from the Holy Spirit is what tells us when we have sinned, even when no one else saw it.

Most of us experience a guilty conscience when we've done something wrong. It's that nagging voice in our heads saying we should have or shouldn't have done something. We may feel like we need to rationalize or justify our behavior, even when we haven't been asked to … yet. We might get defensive if anyone talks about it, but when we think back on how we acted, or what we did in the middle of the situation, we dislike ourselves. We blame ourselves before anyone else even finds out. There's a feeling of guilt we just can't shake.

But there are criminals who have a deadened conscience. Such a conscience just doesn't work properly. It's as if "spiritual scar tissue" has dulled the sense of right and wrong. 1 Timothy 4:2 described it this way. "Now the Spirit speaketh expressly, that in the latter times some shall depart from the faith, giving heed to seducing spirits, and doctrines of devils; speaking lies in hypocrisy; having their conscience seared with a hot iron."

In other words, just as the hide of an animal scarred with a branding iron becomes numb to further pain, so the heart of an individual with a seared conscience is desensitized to morality and a sense of right or wrong. The first time I commit a particular sin, my conscience bothers me. In His grace, the Holy Spirit is convicting me of that lapse. But the more I commit a particular sin, the less it bothers me and the more I can tune out God's input. Eventually I stop feeling any remorse at all about it.

Criminals' consciences become desensitized over time through repetition of their crimes. Depending on their crimes, we may refer to people with such seared consciences as psychopaths or sociopaths, when combined with other key traits. These are the most dangerous of all antisocial personality disorders, because of the way such people can completely dissociate emotionally from their actions, regardless of how terrible those actions may be. We will find examples of such people in the Bible.

1. To what did Timothy compare the conscience of a person who doesn't feel guilty any more when they sin?

(1 Timothy 4:2): 1 Timothy 4:2

[2] speaking lies in hypocrisy, having their own

conscience seared with a hot iron,

Such teachings come through hypocritical liars, whose consciences have been seared as with a hot iron. It is as if the nerve endings of their conscience have been burnt and scarred, and are dead to feeling.

2. This seared conscience is the ultimate result of the process Paul described in Romans 1:28. What is the process?

Romans 1:28

[28] And even as they did not like to retain God in their knowledge, God gave them over to a debased mind, to do those things which are not fitting;

Not retaining the knowledge of God. Exhibit: Furthermore, just as they did not think it worthwhile to retain the knowledge of God, so God gave them over to a depraved mind, so that they do what ought not to be done.

Paul personally knew what it was to have a dead, burned conscience. Before he surrendered his life to Jesus Christ on the road to Damascus, he felt completely justified in his persecution of Christians and hatred of Jesus. He could feel justified because his conscience was seared and needed a wake-up call — which the Lord graciously provided.

3. Following are examples of people in the Bible whose conscience bothered them because they knew they had done something wrong. Who sinned, and what had they done wrong?

a) Genesis 42:21: They said to one another, "Surely, we are being punished because of our brother. We saw how distressed he was when he pleaded with us for his life, but we would not listen; that's why this distress has come on us."

The brothers thought the complicated mess they were in was punishment for the way they had treated Joseph years back. This was a good sign. The quickness with which they associated their current situation with their sin against Joseph so many years before means their conscience had been bothering them about it for years.

b) Exodus 9:27: Then Pharaoh summoned Moses and Aaron. "This time I have sinned," he said to them. "The Lord is in the right, and I and my people are in the wrong.

c) 1 Samuel 24:5: Afterward, David was conscience-stricken for having cut off a corner of his robe.

d) Matthew 27:3-5: 3 When Judas, who had betrayed him, saw that Jesus was condemned, he was seized with remorse and returned the thirty pieces of silver to the chief priests and the elders. 4 "I have sinned," he said, "for I have betrayed innocent blood."

e) Luke 22:61-62: 61 The Lord turned and looked straight at Peter. Then Peter remembered the word the Lord had spoken to him: "Before the rooster crows today, you will disown me three times." 62 And he went outside and wept bitterly.

f) John 8:7-11: 7 When they kept on questioning him, he straightened up and said to them, "Let any one of you who is without sin be the first to throw a stone at her." 8 Again he stooped down and wrote on the ground.

4. Following are examples of people in the Bible with hardened hearts and seared consciences. They didn't lose any sleep at night over their sins. Who were they?

a) Revelation 2:20-21: Jezebel

b) Exodus 1:22: Pharaoh

The root of Pharaoh's hard-heartedness was his pride and arrogance. Even in the face of tremendous proofs and witnessing God's powerful hand at work, Pharaoh's hardened heart caused him to deny the sovereignty of the one, true God.

c) 2 Samuel 18:15-17: Joab

d) Daniel 5:18-20: Nebuchadnezzar

When King Nebuchadnezzar's "heart became arrogant and hardened with pride, he was deposed from his royal throne and stripped of his glory . . . until he acknowledged that the Most High God is sovereign over the kingdoms of men and sets over them anyone He wishes" (Daniel 5:20–21).

e) Judges 16:19-21: Delilah

f) Matthew 2:16: Herod

g) Acts 24:24-27: Felix

Not only pride, but continual and unrepentant sin causes hearts to be hardened. The Bible says that "if we confess our sins, [Jesus] is faithful and just and will forgive us our sins" (1 John 1:9). However, if we don't confess our sins, they have a cumulative and desensitizing effect on the conscience, making it difficult to even distinguish right from wrong.

5. There are people who presume God is so kind and gracious that He would never send anyone to hell. However, what does Paul say will happen to people with hard and impenitent hearts?

(Romans 2:4-5): Or do you despise the riches of His goodness, forbearance, and longsuffering, not knowing that the goodness of God leads you to repentance? 5 But in accordance with your hardness and your impenitent heart you are treasuring up for yourself wrath in the day of wrath and revelation of the righteous judgment of God,

God holds back His wrath out of forbearance and long-suffering. But at the second coming of Jesus the righteous judgment of God will be revealed most clearly.

6. What counsel would you give a person operating under the "I Didn't Do Anything Wrong" thinking error?

Help them to start associate emotionally to their actions, regardless of how terrible those actions may be. By them accepting this, they will be in the healing process and start leaving a life of responsibility

People tend to presume upon the graciousness of God. Instead, they should see the goodness of God and understand:
- God has been better to them than they deserve.
- God has shown them kindness when they have ignored Him.
- God has shown them kindness when they have mocked Him.
- God is not a cruel master and they may safely surrender to Him.

- God is perfectly willing to forgive them.
- God should be served out of simple gratitude.

Unless a person's heart is hardened, when all these things are considered and understood, man will feel compelled to repent and change his ways.

CHAPTER 9

NOTHING SCARES ME

"Nothing Scares Me."

Most felons talk tough and put on a big show of being bold and fearless. They tell themselves and others, "Nothing' scares me, man." They make threats or brag about violent encounters to intimidate and dominate others, but these events may never have actually happened. They block out from their minds the uneasiness that most people experience when they even think of doing something illegal. Somehow, they manage to cut off those feelings of anxiety that prevent the rest of us from doing what we know is wrong.

But the truth is, criminals are afraid no matter what they say or how confident they act, and their fears are widespread, persistent, and intense. They are especially afraid of getting caught, injured, or being put down.

In a study of what criminals feared the most, it was found that 57% of criminals fear an armed victim even more than getting caught by the cops. If they hear a 12-gauge shotgun being racked from behind the door, they will quickly leave.

- 81% of interviewees agreed that a "smart criminal" will try to determine if a potential victim is armed.
- 74% indicated that burglars avoided occupied dwellings, because of fear of being shot. They will come in when you're not home.

- 57% said that most criminals feared armed citizens more than the police.
- 40% of the felons said that they had been deterred from committing a particular crime, because they believed that the potential victim was armed.
- 57% of the felons who had used guns themselves said that they had encountered potential victims who were armed.
- 34% of the criminal respondents said that they had been scared off, shot at, wounded, or captured by an armed citizen.

People on the opposite side of this thinking error will respect God and his laws and turn away from evil. Proverbs 14:16 says, "The wise fear the Lord and shun evil, but a fool is hotheaded and yet feels secure." In other words, hotheaded fools commit crimes in a confident manner, as if no harm will ever come to them. And they gather followers (gang members) who admire their fearless lifestyle and apparent lack of accountability to anyone. We need to counsel such if they don't fear man, they should certainly fear God. When we fear God, all other fears are settled.

1. Read Proverbs 14:16.:

Proverbs 14:16

[16] A wise man fears and departs from evil, But a fool rages and is self-confident.

a) What are the two-character traits of a fool pointed out in this verse?

i): A fool is rages

ii): A fool is self-confident

You can identify a fool both by a person's attitudes and by their actions. The fool has impetuous anger. He is angry against God, for not giving him all he wants and for restricting his life (Proverbs 19:3; Ps 2:1-3; Luke 19:14). He is angry against the righteous, for living a more holy life than his (Mark 15:10; Ecclesiastes 4:4; Acts 13:45). He is angry against authority, for he refuses to obey others (Proverbs 21:9; 2 Peter 2:10-12; Deuteronomy 21:20).

b) What are the two-character traits of a wise man pointed out in this verse?

i): fears

ii): and departs from evil

A wise man has fear. He has reverent fear of God, which is the beginning of wisdom and the whole duty of man (Proverbs 9:10; Ecclesiastes 12:13; Psalm 111:10). He fears his own heart, for he knows how wicked it is (Psalm 19:12-13; 51:10; 119:36; Jeremiah 17:9). He fears authority, for God has put others over him (Proverbs 24:21; Ecclesiastes 8:1-5; Ephesians 6:1-3,5-8; I Peter 3:1-2; Hebrews 13:17).

Job also taught this lesson with similar words in Job 28:28.

2. According to Psalm 128:1, who will be blessed?

Blessed is everyone who fears the Lord, who walks in His ways.

A fool's impetuous nature causes him to be confident in doing evil. He believes he is right and nothing will happen to him (Proverbs 7:22; 14:12; 26:12). Nothing scares him/her. There is no glory in such confidence – it is a horrible sin based in scorn, pride, stubbornness, and rebellion.

3. What three pieces of advice does the Lord give us in Proverbs 3:7?

Proverbs 3:7

7 Do not be wise in your own eyes;

Fear the LORD and depart from evil.

a): Do not be wise in your own eyes;

b): Fear the Lord

c): and depart from evil.

And these three fundamental steps are connected. We know nothing apart from God's revelation, and the sooner we learn this fact, the sooner we are on the road to wisdom (I Corinthians 3:18-20). We will not fear God until we crush our pride and despise our own personal brand of wisdom. And we will not despise sin and this world until we rightly fear the Lord (Psalm 4:4).

4. Read Proverbs 9:10 and Psalm 111:10. What is the starting place of all wisdom and knowledge? The fear of the Lord

Proverbs 9:10

10 "The fear of the LORD is the beginning of wisdom, And the knowledge of the Holy One is understanding.

Psalm 111:10

10 The fear of the LORD is the beginning of wisdom; A good understanding have all those who do His commandments. His praise endures forever.

5. What advice did Solomon give in Ecclesiastes 12:13 that applies to every man?

Ecclesiastes 12:13

13 Let us hear the conclusion of the whole matter: Fear God and keep His commandments, for this is man's all.
a): Fear God

Fearing God causes us to put Him in first place, and all our personal fears, hopes, and desires in their proper place.
b): and keep His commandments

6. Solomon's definition of the fear of God in Proverbs is to hate evil. What are some corresponding actions we will demonstrate in our lives when we fear God and hate evil?

a): Reverence of God

b): Love Him {God} and exercise the graces of the Spirit

c): Faith in Jesus Christ

For the unbeliever, the fear of God is the fear of the judgment of God and eternal death, which is eternal separation from God (Luke 12:5; Hebrews 10:31).

For the believer, the fear of God is something much different. The believer's fear is reverence of God. Hebrews 12:28-29 is a good description of this: "Therefore, since we are receiving a kingdom that cannot be shaken, let us be thankful, and so worship God acceptably with reverence and awe, for our 'God is a consuming fire.'" This reverence and awe is exactly what the fear of God means for Christians. This is the motivating factor for us to surrender to the Creator of the Universe.

7. Read Job 1:1. How is Job described in this verse?

Job 1:1

New King James Version

Job and His Family in Uz

1 There was a man in the land of Uz, whose name was Job; and that man was blameless and upright, and one who feared God and shunned evil.

Blameless and upright, and one who feared God and shunned evil.

8. Although Job was a godly man, his friends thought he must be guilty of some unconfessed sin. What did Zophar say would be the result if he would just confess and repent?

a) Job 11:18: And you would be secure, because there is hope; Yes, you would dig around you, and take your rest in safety.

b) Job 11:19: You would also lie down, and no one would make you afraid; Yes, many would court your favor.

Job's friends were certain that Job must have sinned in order to deserve punishment and argued with him about it. But Job maintained his innocence, though he confessed that he wanted to die and did ask God about everything that had happened.

Our responsibility to God is to obey Him, to trust Him, and to submit to His will, whether we understand it or not. When we do, we will find God in the midst of our trials—possibly even because of our trials. We will see more clearly the magnificence of our God, and we will say, with Job, "My ears had heard of you but now my eyes have seen you" (Job 42:5).

c) Would this be good advice for a criminal who can't sleep at night because of fear or a guilty conscience? Yes

d) Explain your answer.: If the criminals are guilty conscience, it is the beginning of their way to freedom, because through guiltiness within, they may be able to search and or seek God and ask forgiveness. Jesus is waiting for that time for them to repent and accept Him.

Confession of sin will help to keep us from the discipline of the Lord. If we fail to confess sin, the discipline of the Lord is sure to come until we do confess it. Our sins are forgiven at salvation (positional forgiveness), but our daily fellowship with God needs to stay in good standing (relational forgiveness). Proper fellowship with God cannot happen with unconfessed sin in our lives. Therefore, we need to confess our sins to God as soon as we are aware that we have sinned, in order to maintain close fellowship with God.

9. According to the scriptures quoted above, instead of fearing a victim with a gun or the police, whom should a criminal fear? God

10. Fearing God means to understand that there are consequences for disobedience. This is not because He is mean or vindictive, but it is simply because when we disobey, our disobedience ushers us out from under His covering of protection. His standard still stands today as a plumb line for all generations. Yet, although He is a just God, because of His mercy and compassion, ... (Romans 3:26-28): Therefore, we conclude that a man is justified by faith apart from the deeds of the law.

11. How would you counsel a person operating under the "Nothing Scares Me" thinking error?

Help such individual to admit that they are in fear and needs help. Once they are will to admit their fears, I will help him by first introducing Jesus to their life who is the answer for everything.

And, besides fearing God, a criminal should fear the consequences of his/her lifestyle. The average life of a street level drug dealer is around 3 to 5 years. If they're not dead in that time, they're usually in prison.

CHAPTER 10

I CAN'T HELP IT

"I Can't Help It."

People with this thinking error will tell you they can't help the way they act, that's the way they're wired. Their excuse implies you'll just have to accept their bad behavior, forgive them anyway, and not expect them to change. Often, when living with someone who says this, others around will actually offer more excuses than the person himself (herself) does.

- "That's just the way he is."
- "He can't help himself."
- "You know he's got a short fuse."
- "That's the way her mother was."
- "He's having problems at work." "
- "He's always been that way."
- "She's under a lot of stress,"
- "She just acts/reacts without thinking first."
- "He doesn't know any better."
- "Such-and-such just happened, and she's taking it out on you."
- "He's just in a bad mood."

These are just some of the lame excuses offered to explain unacceptable behavior. In the case of an abuser, it's the wife who typically makes the most excuses, even though, paradoxically, she will also complain more about his behavior than anyone else.

There was a 62-year old pedophile who was finally arrested and sent to prison after 25 years of raping and molesting dozens of little boys. His wife knew he was a pedophile because he had spent two years molesting her own child, covered for him, and even babysat other people's children and left them alone with him. When he was finally caught, the wife said, "He has the mentality of a 14-year old", followed by, "He's very immature and thinks he's on the same level as the children he rapes." In other words, he couldn't help himself.

Well, nice try. This is just more hogwash invented by self-centered people and their enablers to allow them to get away with murder, so to speak. And it puts the victim in an impossible position. How can we expect people who claim they can't control themselves, that they can't help it when they do things that are wrong, to be able to respect our own boundaries and limits?

1. One of the perils all people face day to day is temptation. Where do temptations to sin come from?

a) Matthew 4:3: Satan: Now when the tempter came to Him, he said, "If You are the Son of God, command that these stones become bread."

And note that Matthew referred to the devil by his function—the tempter.

b) 1 John 2:16: For all that is in the world—the lust of the flesh, the lust of the eyes, and the pride of life—is not of the Father but is of the world.

Satan always tempts us to move into human viewpoint exclusive of divine viewpoint. The devil seeks to tempt us to find resource in something other than God or His Word. His timing in this is when we are at our weakest.

c) James 1:14-15: 14 But each one is tempted when he is drawn away by his own desires and enticed. 15 Then, when desire has conceived, it gives birth to sin; and sin, when it is full-grown, brings forth death.

When we start considering a temptation, and imagining how much we would enjoy it, it becomes our own evil desire.

2. Is it possible these excuses are valid – that we just can't help but sin when drawn into or tempted by certain situations? It's our nature to sin, isn't it? Even when we know the consequences, we still do it. What does God say?

a) 1 Corinthians 10:13: No temptation has overtaken you except such as is common to man; but God is faithful, who will not allow you to be tempted beyond what you are able, but with the temptation will also make the way of escape, that you may be able to bear it.

b) Romans 13:14: But put on the Lord Jesus Christ, and make no provision for the flesh, to fulfill its lusts.

c) Hebrews 12:1: Therefore, we also, since we are surrounded by so great a cloud of witnesses, let us lay aside every weight, and the sin which so easily ensnares us, and let us run with endurance the race that is set before us,

d) Galatians 5:16: I say then: Walk in the Spirit, and you shall not fulfill the lust of the flesh.

Jesus demonstrated the way God expects us to respond to temptation (Matthew 4), no matter what the source. Notice how He responded to all three temptations with … "It is written …" It is the Word of God that sustains dynamic fellowship with God. Dependence on God depends on knowing the Word of God. Just as physical food goes into our body and converts into energy, so taking in the Word of God converts into spiritual energy and power.

3. Instead of thinking up reasons (excuses) to accept her offer, list some of the things Joseph did to help himself remain faithful to God and Potiphar in this situation.:

a): look, my master does not know what is with me in the house,

b): and he has committed all that he has to my hand.

c): There is no one greater in this house than I,

d): nor has he kept back anything from me but you, because you are his wife.

e): How then can I do this great wickedness,

f): and sin against God?

The story of Joseph is a good example of a man living a disciplined life. Too many of us think we have the strength to face down temptations from the middle of the situation. Joseph shows us when it is good to make a stand, and when it is better to remove ourselves from people who lack self-discipline.

4. Our Father in his infinite mercy does not expect us to patiently listen to the excuses people give us for sinning, and continue tolerating abuse with no hope of it ever ending. What two things does He tell us to do in Luke 17:3?

Luke 17:3

[3] Take heed to yourselves. If your brother sins [a]against you, rebuke him; and if he repents, forgive him.

a): If your brother sins against you, rebuke him;

b): and if he repents, forgive him.

5. What does Titus 3:10-11 say we are to do after we have warned a person two times? To reject a divisive man

Titus 3:10-11

[10] Reject a divisive man after the first and second admonition, [11] knowing that such a person is warped and sinning, being self-condemned.

This is backed up in 2 Thessalonians 3:14: "And if any man obey not our word by this epistle, note that man, and have no company with him, that he may be ashamed."

6. Matthew 18:15-17 gives step-by-step instructions for dealing with people who sin against us, won't accept responsibility for it, don't repent, and refuse to change.:

Matthew 18:15-17

Dealing with a Sinning Brother

[15] "Moreover if your brother sins against you, go and tell him his fault between you and him alone. If he hears you, you have gained your brother. [16] But if he will not hear, take with you one or two more, that 'by the mouth of two or three witnesses every word may be established.' [17] And if he refuses to hear them, tell it to the church. But if he refuses even to hear the church, let him be to you like a heathen and a tax collector

a): go and tell him his fault between you and him alone.

b): But if he will not hear, take with you one or two more, that 'by the mouth of two or three witnesses every word may be established.'

c): And if he refuses to hear them, tell it to the church.

d): But if he refuses even to hear the church, let him be to you like a heathen and a tax collector.

7. According to 2 Timothy 3: 5, what should we do when we find ourselves in the company of people who pretend to be devoted to God and who make a show of religion, but behind the scenes they live the way they want - with handy excuses ready if you challenge them on their behavior? To turn away from such people.

2 Timothy 3:5

[5] having a form of godliness but denying its power. And from such people turn away!

Having a form of godliness but denying its power. And from such people turn away!

When ministering to prisoners, this is an important lesson to impart. If an ex-con is going to change his/her lifestyle and stay out of prison, he/she will have to make new friends - friends that will exercise self-discipline. They must learn that not everyone is headed in the right direction. As a matter of fact, many are not even on the right road. They will need to learn to recognize and seek out believers who are actually walking their talk as mentors and friends.

8. How would you counsel a person operating under the "I Can't Help It" thinking error?
Tell them to stop giving lame excuses and start dealing with their issues.

Since Adam and Eve, God has held us accountable for our choices and behavior.

- Adam's son Cain was warned by God that he would be held personally responsible for his actions (Genesis 4:7).
- Achan was held responsible for his sin at Jericho (Joshua 7:14–15).
- Jonah was held responsible for his choice to run from the Lord (Jonah 1:7–8).
- The Levites were held responsible for the care of the tabernacle (Numbers 18:5).
- The deacons of the early church took personal responsibility for meeting some practical needs of the church (Acts 6:3).
- Paul was given the responsibility to blaze a gospel trail to the Gentiles (Ephesians 3:2).

The Bible clearly teaches that Lord expects us to accept personal responsibility for all areas of our lives. The excuse "I can't help it" is not acceptable to Him.

CHAPTER 11

I AM ABOVE THE LAW

"I'm Above the Law."

You may never had heard anyone say this out loud, but most lifestyle criminals believe that they are entitled to violate the laws of society and the rights of others. They believe that the laws don't actually apply to them. And the more they get away with breaking the law, the more they do it.

Before you get on your high horse and say, "I would never do such a thing," examine your own conscience. Have you ever under-reported your income when you submitted your taxes? Did you ever over-claim your expenses? Sometimes we feel "entitled" to do this because we don't approve of the way the government spends our tax dollars. Or we think we already pay too much in taxes anyway. But if you're audited, and investigators determine you willfully defrauded the government, you could be looking at 75% in penalties plus jail time.

As drivers, we've all subconsciously considered ourselves to be above the law at some point in time. Have you ever parked in a no parking zone or a handicap spot, because you're "just going to be gone a minute"? When a traffic light turned yellow, did you ever punch the gas and breeze on through the "pink" light instead of slowing down to stop? Did you ever roll through a stop sign without making a complete stop, if no one was around? Have you ever gone over the speed limit because you were running late, or because everyone else was going a zillion mph over? When you were younger, did you ever get behind the wheel after a few too many drinks thinking, "I can drive myself home; I'm not really drunk"? Many of us have routinely broken traffic laws without seeing any consequences and thought, "If no one gets hurt, does it really matter?"

In other words, it's not just criminals that operate under this thinking error. We've been guilty of this as well. But the fact is, no one is above the law, any law … not a high-ranking politician, not a priest, not a police officer, not a millionaire, not a celebrity, not a lawyer, and certainly not criminals. We are all accountable for our actions.

From a Biblical perspective, submission is the proper response of the believer to those who in a position of authority over us. We are to obey man's laws as though they are God's laws. Submission to civil authorities facilitates the task God has given to those who govern, to punish the wicked and protect the righteous.

Human government was instituted by God after the Genesis flood. The key verse is Genesis 9:6 which says that the person who sheds man's blood (violent murder), by man shall his blood be shed. God could have Himself punished murderers directly, but instead He chose to delegate this responsibility to man. Human government is instituted and ordained by God, and whether saved or unsaved, all men benefit from government and all men ought to fear the government if they disobey its laws and rebel against its authority.

1. Read 1 Peter 2:13-15.:
1 Peter 2:13-15
Submission to Government-

[13] Therefore submit yourselves to every [a]ordinance of man for the Lord's sake, whether to the king as supreme, [14] or to governors, as to those who are sent by him for the punishment of evildoers and for the praise of those who do good. [15] For this is the

will of God, that by doing good you may put to silence the ignorance of foolish men—

a) To whom is the believer to submit? to every ordinance of man for the Lord's sake,

Peter wrote this in the days of the Roman Empire, which was not a democracy and no special friend to Christians. Yet he still recognized the legitimate authority of the Roman government.

b) Why are we to submit to the authorities mentioned above? For this is the will of God,

As Christians we should be good citizens, submitting to our federal, state, and local governments. This was very different from the zealous Jews in Peter's Day who recognized no king but God and argues that they shouldn't have to pay taxes to anyone except God.

c) Who raises up leaders? God

Since governments have a rightful authority from God, we are bound to obey them – unless, of course, they order us to do something in contradiction to God's law. Then, we are commanded to obey God before man (Acts 4:19).

d) For what purpose are do we have government authorities? for the punishment of evildoers and for the praise of those who do good.

God uses governing authorities as a check upon man's sinful desires and tendencies. Based also on what Paul wrote in Romans 13, we can say that the greatest offense government can make is to fail to punish evildoers, or to reward evildoers through corruption.

2. According to Ephesians 5:21, why are we to obey the law?

Ephesians 5:21

[21] submitting to one another in the fear of God.

"Submitting" was a Greek military term that meant to rank under. If there is anything important in the military, it is the idea of authority and following lines of authority. An army cannot function without authority. Soldiers must accept the authority of the officers over them. A disorderly army is an army that is in disarray.

Likewise, a country with citizens who do not obey the law will be a country in disarray.   And a church that does not accept the authority of its leaders will be a church in disarray (Hebrews 13:17).
3. Read Romans 13:1-7.:

Romans 13:1-7

Submit to Government-

13 Let every soul be subject to the governing authorities. For there is no authority except from God, and the authorities that exist are appointed by God. [a] Therefore whoever resists the authority resists the ordinance of God, and those who resist will [a]bring judgment on themselves. [3] For rulers are not a terror to good works, but to evil. Do you want to be unafraid of the authority? Do what is good, and you will have praise from the same. [4] For he is God's minister to you for good. But if you do evil, be afraid; for he does not bear the sword in vain; for he is God's minister, an avenger to execute wrath on him who practices evil. [5] Therefore you must be subject, not only because of wrath but also for conscience' sake. [6] For because of this you also pay taxes, for they are God's ministers attending continually to this very thing. [7] Render therefore to all their due: taxes to whom taxes are due, customs to whom customs, fear to whom fear, honor to whom honor.

a) When a man rebels against civil authorities, against whom is he also rebelling? God. Exhibit: For there is no authority except from God, and the authorities that exist are appointed by God.

b) What happens as a result of this rebellion? (vs. 2): whoever resists the authority resists the ordinance of God, and those who resist will bring judgment on themselves.

c) How do we get rid of our fear of the governmental authorities? (vs. 3): Do what is good, and you will have praise from the same.

d) What are the governmental authorities called in verse 4? God's minister

e) What therefore is the responsibility of the governmental authorities? (vs.

4): an avenger to execute wrath on him who practices evil.

f) Besides fearing what the government might do to you if the police catch you doing something wrong, what is the other reason we are to submit to the government? (vs. 5): also for conscience' sake

g) According to verse 6, what is the purpose of taxes? for they are God's ministers attending continually to this very thing.

h) How does Paul say we should handle paying our taxes? (vs. 7): Render therefore to all their due: taxes to whom taxes are due, customs to whom customs, fear to whom fear, honor to whom honor.

The tension is that the Christian is the citizen of two kingdoms, an earthly government and a heavenly kingdom (Matthew 22:15-22; Philippians 3:20; Colossians 1:13).

The principles for God's empowerment of the state are found in Romans 13:1-5:

- Christians are to submit to the state, 1:1a
- The state has its authority from divine establishment, 1:1b
- Rebellion against the state is mutiny against both God and government, 1:2a
- God and the state will punish those who violate law, 1:2b
- The state constrains evil, 1:3a
- The state serves social order, 1:3-4a
- God delegates the state power to punish lawbreakers, 1:4b
- The Christian should let his conscience obey the state, 1:5

4. What did Jesus say we should do regarding the tax dollars we owe the government in Luke 20:25? Render therefore to Caesar the things that are Caesar's

Luke 20:25 And He said to them, "Render therefore to Caesar the things that are Caesar's, and to God the things that are God's."

The word "render" means to give back. This presupposes that what we pay to government in taxes presumes a value has been received. There is an obligation we owe to the state. What is "due" not only includes taxes but also respect for the principle of governmental order.

5. What did Paul tell Titus he should do in Titus 3:1?
Remind them to be subject to rulers and authorities, to obey, to be ready for every good work,

6. What does 1 John 2:4 say about a person who claims they know God but also breaks the law?
Is a liar, and the truth is not in him.

It is possible to obey laws and not fellowship with God, but keeping His commandments demonstrates the reality of that fellowship with God.

7. a) Is there anyone who is above the law?
No. We are all accountable for our actions no matter who you are or your position.

8. How would you counsel a person operating under the "I'm Above the Law" thinking error?
Remind them that no one is above the law, any law. We are all subjected to it and we should to our best to keep all laws.

I think believers in the U.S. feel especially justified in "breaking the law" when they cheat on their income tax returns. But, in our scriptures for this lesson, we can see that giving the government part of our income is a way we can honor the Lord and express our trust in his grand design. Scripture points us to a view of taxation that is intrinsically connected to our obedience to God.

CHAPTER 12

HE ONLY GOT WHAT HE DESERVED

"He Only Got What He Deserved."

Offenders make moral judgments about their own behavior and often rationalize their conduct to "neutralize" what would otherwise be incapacitating feelings of guilt or shame. For example, if they cause physical harm to someone, they may make such excuses as: "He deserved it," "I only slapped her," "He had it coming," "He brought it on himself," She was just asking for it."

This excuse may even be a maxim by which they live, to justify angry outbursts when they settle matters with their fists … or a knife … or a gun. Such a person may appear to be out of control, but they are often using their anger quite purposefully, to remind other people that it is dangerous to cross them. In other words, such actions may be intended to control others.

By contrast, both Christians and morally sensitive non-Christians have trouble with the word "deserve." This is why the grading system in schools today is in a shambles. There is a growing reluctance to reward good work with good grades and bad work with bad grades. Teachers and principals try to avoid saying, "Johnny deserved to fail."

Regarding salaries, there is an aversion to the idea of paying people differently according to the merit of their work. They simply can't say, "Employee A deserves more money than employee B because his work is better." They pay by seniority or job title, routinely give a cost-of-living raise about once a year, but seldom give raises based on the quality of the job being done.

We no longer have penal institutions. Instead, we call them correctional institutions. This implies that we no longer punish our criminals; we re-educate them. No one wants to ask, "What does a thief deserve?" We would rather ask, "How can we reshape his thinking so that he doesn't do that again?"

Whether you live by the word "deserve," as do violent criminals or abusive spouses, or if you avoid that word altogether - the Biblical truth is, those of us who are believers in Jesus Christ, and His finished work on the cross, will never get what we "deserve." If we have ever sinned, our just fate is eternal damnation. But by grace, through faith, we have been forgiven and will enjoy eternal life in heaven.

1. Is there anyone besides Jesus who has lived a perfect life without sin? How do these verses answer that question?

a) Isaiah 53:6: WE ARE ALL SINNERS: All we like sheep have gone astray; we have turned everyone to his own way; and the Lord hath laid on him the iniquity of us all.

Sheep are stupid, headstrong animals, that want to go their own way. And we, like sheep, want to do our own thing, go our own way. At some point in our lives, we have all turned against God's way, to go own way.

b) Isaiah 64:6: But we are all as an unclean thing, and all our righteous nesses are as filthy rags; and we all do fade as a leaf; and our iniquities, like the wind, have taken us away.

I always thought this verse referred to worn-out, dirty clothes - such as a homeless person would wear. But the term "filthy rags" actually refers to "a garment of menstruation." Bodily discharges were considered a defilement because they were the outflow of a sinful, fallen human nature.

In other words, Isaiah is saying that even our righteous works that we might think would tip the scales in our favor are defiled.

c) Ecclesiastes 7:20: For there is not a just man upon earth, that doeth good, and sinneth not.

d) Psalm 130:3-5: 3 If thou, Lord, shouldest mark iniquities, O Lord, who shall stand? 4 But there is forgiveness with thee, that thou mayest be feared. 5 I wait for the Lord, my soul doth wait, and in his word do, I hope.

e) 1 John 1:8-10: 8 If we say that we have no sin, we deceive ourselves, and the truth is not in us.

There were Christians in John's Day who erroneously contended that they had no guilt due to their sin. They were listening to Cerinthus, a false teacher living in Ephesus, who gave them the fake news that they didn't need to accept guilt for their sin. And there are still false teachers today with great personalities who are able to communicate effectively. They are normally charismatic and likeable people. That is the primary reason Bible believing Christians fall for this false teaching.

Rebellion against God's truth always leads us into self-deception and error. We are fooling no one but ourselves. We need to be honest about the sin that is in our lives so that we can deal with it effectively.

f) Romans 3:22-25: 2 Even the righteousness of God which is by faith of Jesus Christ unto all and upon all them that believe: for there is no difference:

This is the reason men cannot stand before God on their own merit. There is no person who never sinned except Jesus.

The only means of salvation is faith through grace. God had to make this provision or man's sinfulness would prohibit him from being saved. God demands perfection of Himself and of us. If He were to accept anything less, heaven would fill with characters contradictory to His own nature. Heaven would no longer be heaven in that case.

2. There were self-righteous people in the Bible who claimed they were leading a sinless life without transgressions. Who were they?

a) Luke 15:29: Our own Children, like this brother of the prodigal son

b) Luke 18:11-12: Pharisees

3. Why did Jesus have to be sacrificed? (Romans 6:23; Ezekiel 18:4): Because the gift of God is eternal life through Jesus Christ our Lord.

4. Why didn't God on one clear day in eternity simply say, For God so loved the world, that he gave his only begotten Son, that whosoever believeth in him should not perish, but have everlasting life.

a) When the high priest decided that Jesus had committed blasphemy, he asked the people what they thought Jesus deserved for that. How did they answer? (Matthew 26:66): They answered and said, He is guilty of death.

Their verdict revealed the depths of man's depravity. God, in total perfection, came to earth, lived among men, and this was man's reply to God.

b) What was Pilate's verdict? (Luke 23:4): I find no fault in this man.

Even though Pilate was a cruel, ruthless man he wasn't oblivious to what was going on behind his back. He could see through the motives of the religious leaders and had no problem in validating Jesus and the whole situation by the declaration, "I find no fault in this Man."

c) Pilate was willing to release Jesus, but what did the Jewish leaders and the crowd insist that Jesus deserved? (Luke 23:21): they cried, saying, crucify him, crucify him.

d) It was obvious to Pilate that a riot was building. And so, to please the people, he did as they asked. What did Jesus really deserve? As Pilate said previously that he found no fault on Jesus and should have released Him, in contrast, Jesus had to be crucified in order to fulfil the Word.

6. When we sin, do we get what we deserve? How do the following Bible verses answer this question?

This is an easy one to answer. We don't deserve to be loved. But for some reason, God DOES love us. Just think back to what the Word of God says about those who belong to Him. We are the apple of His eye, He rejoices over us, He sings over us, He abounds in love over us, He has the compassion of a Father over us, He delights over us … and His love is from everlasting to everlasting.

And we don't deserve to be forgiven. But God tells us in dozens of Scriptures that He will forgive us willingly if we will just believe in the saving work of His Son, Jesus Christ.

a) Psalm 103:10: He hath not dealt with us after our sins; nor rewarded us according to our iniquities.

b) Romans 4:5: But to him that worketh not, but believeth on him that justifieth the ungodly, his faith is counted for righteousness.

c) Galatians 3:13: Christ hath redeemed us from the curse of the law, being made a curse for us: for it is written, cursed is every one that hangeth on a tree:

d) Acts 2:21: And it shall come to pass, that whosoever shall call on the name of the Lord shall be saved.

e) Romans 10:9: That if thou shalt confess with thy mouth the Lord Jesus, and shalt believe in thine heart that God hath raised him from the dead, thou shalt be saved.

Confession is public identification with Christ as the Messiah. The Greek word means to say the same thing. Confession with the "mouth" indicates that the confession must be made audibly and openly. This is a confession that, as Lord, Christ as God is sovereign over all things, especially sovereign over our salvation.

7. If salvation were the only blessing, we ever received from God, it would be so much more than we deserve. But after we are saved by grace through faith, we become the adopted children of God. And the Lord loves to shower His children with blessings above and beyond salvation. List of the blessings God has given to you beyond salvation, blessings you don't really deserve.:

a): The Lord blessed me with health, I never got sick or ill for over ten years.

b): One time I lost my car due to age, but God supplied a new Benz ML 320. It was amazing because I did not expect my Muslim friend to do that, but God touched him and he did it

c): In the year 2016 I received supernatural financial monies in my business account, it was $96,000

If salvation were the only blessing, we ever received from God, it would be much more than we deserve. But after we are saved by grace through faith, we become the adopted children of God. And the Lord loves to shower His children with "Blessings Above and Beyond" our most precious gift of salvation.

A question for the reader: How would you counsel a person operating under the "He/she deserved it" thinking error?

CHAPTER 13

NO ONE WILL EVER KNOW

"No One Will Ever Know."

Criminals are often very secretive. By keeping secrets and sustaining an air of mystery about their comings and goings, they maintain power and control over others. Many criminals believe that if they tell their secrets, if another person gets to know them intimately, they will no longer have power over them.

Others keep secrets because of a fear of rejection. For recovering addicts, it can be embarrassing and intimate to reveal struggles with substance abuse. Someone who is still actively hopped up on narcotics will keep that a secret, because they may be afraid you will turn them in. Sex offenders are the most likely to keep their past a secret, due to the heavy shame and stigma around sex crimes.

On the most basic level, criminals are secretive about their crimes of opportunity. They may see a dangling purse or an unlocked car. They aren't thinking about consequences because they don't expect to get caught. They figure they'll be in and back out before you know what happened. You'll never find out it was them.

Secrecy is a big part of gangs. They get very upset if outsiders somehow get inside information about the way they operate. They like the sense of belonging, the sense of community, the idea that others don't see things the way we do. They like the power, the connectedness, that feeling of finally fitting in and having a purpose. That is what keeps the gang going, and they don't want the secrets of their club to be exposed.

With regard to organized crime, these unlawful acts are well coordinated and planned out in advance. At this level, there is experience and practiced precautions, all the team members have an awareness of the risks, and would never divulge the actions of the others. If they did, they might be killed. Undercover agents who try to infiltrate the organization may also be killed before they can disclose what they learned.

If there's a criminal living next door, he is probably leading a double life. There will be a secretive dimension to his comings and goings. He won't want his neighbors to know what he's up to – even when he is just going about his daily business. How many times have you heard about an arrest on the news, and all the neighbors said the same thing. "We were so surprised to hear this about Mr. Smith. He was such a quiet neighbor, always polite. We never imagined he would/could do such a thing."

1. What are some of the things a criminal is likely to keep a secret?
a): Their operation.
b): Their struggles with substance abuse/narcotics.
c): Their Sex offences.
d): Secretive about their crimes of opportunity.

You might say such people have learned how to successfully lead double lives - the one we can see, and the one they keep hidden. A surprising example is found in the life of Charles Lindbergh. From piloting the first solo nonstop transatlantic flight in 1927 to the "trial of the century" surrounding the kidnapping and murder of his eldest son, the 6'3" man could scarcely step outside without being mobbed.

And yet, it turns out that Lindbergh traveled back and forth for 20 years between his American wife and six kids and the multiple children he fathered out of wedlock with three European women, including a Munich hat-maker — and her sister. And, in spite of being a public figure, somehow, he managed to keep it all a secret.

2. We may be able to hide our double life and secret sins from others, but can we hide from these things God? How do each of these verses answer that question?

a) Numbers 32:23: But if ye will not do so, behold, ye have sinned against the Lord: and be sure your sin will find you out.

b) Hebrews 4:13: Neither is there any creature that is not manifest in his sight: but all things are naked and opened unto the eyes of him with whom we have to do.

c) 1 Samuel 16:7: But the Lord said unto Samuel, Look not on his countenance, or on the height of his stature; because I have refused him: for the Lord seeth not as man seeth; for man looketh on the outward appearance, but the Lord looketh on the heart.

d) Luke 12:2-3: 2 For there is nothing covered, that shall not be revealed; neither hid, that shall not be known.

Your sins will surely be found out.

- A hidden sin shows up on your face (Isaiah 3:9). Did your mom ever say to you, "I know you did it. It's written all over your face!"
- Sin will show up in your body (1 Corinthians 11:30). Sin, and the stress of hiding the sin, can lead to sickness, although not all sickness comes from sin.
- Sin may be revealed in your children' lives (Exodus 20:5). For example, King David's sin resulted in his own child's death.
- Sin shows up in a guilty conscience (Psalm 51:3). Without repentance, eventually people's minds are affected by sin to the point that they can no longer tell right from wrong. That is a reprobate mind.

• Sin will be revealed in the judgment (Romans 14:12, 2nd Corinthians 5:10). Eventually we will all have to give an accounting of our lives.

3. Read Genesis 3.:

a) Who were the first persons who tried to hide their sins? Adam and Eve

b) What was their sin? They ate the forbidden fruit [knowing good and evil.

c) How did God respond? And He said, Who told thee that thou wast naked? Hast thou eaten of the tree, whereof I commanded thee that thou shouldest not eat?

But thankfully, God did not abandon Adam and Eve. He provided clothing for them (Genesis 3:21) and allowed them to have children (Genesis 4). He also promised "the seed of the woman" to crush the power of the serpent (Genesis 3:15). This promise was fulfilled in Jesus Christ, who defeated sin and death on the cross and provides abundant life now (John 10:10) and eternal life with God in heaven (John 3:16). As Romans 5:19 says, "For as by the one man's [Adam's] disobedience the many were made sinners, so by the one man's [Jesus'] obedience the many will be made righteous."

4. What will God one day judge?

a) Ecclesiastes 12:14: For God shall bring every work into judgment, with every secret thing, whether it be good, or whether it be evil.

b) Romans 2:16: In the day when God shall judge the secrets of men by Jesus Christ according to my gospel.

Many people wear a "mask" before others. God's judgment will strip this false façade from them and they will be seen for what they are in the day of God's judgment. And God will judge our motives as well as our overt actions.

5. No sin, not even a whispered curse or a fleeting evil thought, is hidden from the view of God. 1 Samuel 16:7 tells us "God sees not as man sees ...:

a) for man looks at the outward appearance,

Even though we know better, we tend to judge people based on their outward appearances. In other words, we're judging the heart that we can't see based on a person's clothes or good looks.
b) but the Lord looks at the heart

But God … He is not swayed by appearances, but is focused on knowing what is going on in our hearts The seat of our passions and deepest desires reflects what matters most to us; it shows what we're willing to live and die for.

6. It is the very height of foolishness to convince ourselves that we can get away with sin by covering it up. What does Proverbs 28:13 say about those who try? He that covereth his sins shall not prosper: but whoso confesseth and forsaketh them shall have mercy.

7. All sin is an assault against our holy God, whether it is done in public or in secret. And God, Who sees even the innermost secrets of the heart, views our sin clearly, no matter how well we think we have covered it. Don't let unconfessed, secret sins come between you and God. In 1 John 1:9, what wonderful promise is given to believers?

If we confess our sins, he is faithful and just to forgive us our sins, and to cleanse us from all unrighteousness.

8. Your secret life is the true ultimate test of your character. What you do when no one else is looking is the best measure of your integrity. Do you want to know who you really are?

Take a hard look at your private life, especially your innermost secret thoughts. Proverbs 23:7 says ...: or as he thinketh in his heart, so is he: Eat and drink, saith he to thee; but his heart is not with thee.

And this is an unchanging, divine principle: in order to live right we must first think right.

9. How would you counsel a person operating under the "No One Will Ever Know" thinking error?

Start with prayer and ask God to guide you prior to speaking to the individual. Let the person know that, nothing is hidden in the eyes of God, so confessing our sins is the best way pursuant to Proverbs 28:13. In all my counseling I will follow the infallible Word guidance.

And remind them God knows … and He's patiently waiting for them to repent, confess the secret sin, and move forward with Him. I think, in many cases, this will require a godly accountability partner, because a secret sin is difficult to let go.

CHAPTER 14

I WON'T

"I Won't."

A person who refuses to obey the law, likes to challenge authority and flout regulations, and frequently crosses the line of acceptable behavior may enjoy watching the frustration grow within others. Such a person will often get very quiet, and decline to explain their position or reason for refusing to do what is lawful or expected. It generates within themselves a feeling of silent power over others.

Disrespect for the law and refusal to obey has become common in America, and started at the top. The Obama administration announced it will no longer enforce immigration laws. Secretary of Homeland Security, Janet Napolitano, has suspended deportation proceedings and is granting amnesty to those who appear to fit the criteria of the Dream Act – a bill that was defeated with the overwhelming support of Congress. By this, our leaders have declared to the country that our laws will <u>not</u> be executed faithfully.

What sort of message does this convey to our citizens, especially our youth, regarding the inviolability of the rule of law? With our leadership flouting the law, how can we expect the man on the street to have respect for those who enforce the law?

Disrespect for and refusal to obey law enforcement officers has become so common that there is a new term used to label it … "contempt of cop." The phrase is a play on the words "contempt of court", and refers to people who challenge authority and refuse to obey police officers. The "Black Lives Matter" movement developed as a protest against the actions police have taken when a black person was killed who appeared to be threatening the life of another. Cops are being killed as a result, and in response there is now a movement called "Blue Lives Matter."

The spirit of anarchy is permeating all nations, not just America. We are living in an epidemic of crime, with so many refusing to obey their country's laws. Too many are like a rebellious Rubik's Cube – no matter which way you try to turn them, you can never get them going in the right direction, doing the right thing.

Thousands are living in transgression of God's laws as well as their government's laws. And this isn't just a legal issue - it's also a spiritual issue. The absolute holiness of God demands a standard of holiness and obedience from those who worship Him. He has expressly commanded this of His people: "Ye shall be holy for I, the Lord your God, am holy" (Leviticus 19:2; 20:26).

God is holy. In order to please Him, nothing less than holiness will do. God commanded Israel, through Moses, to obey His commands completely and worship Him exclusively

1. a) As you have read through the Old Testament, did you find that the Israelites were obedient? Did they worship Him exclusively? (Judges 2:10-13): No

Judges 2:10-13

[10] When all that generation hadbeen gathered to their fathers, another generation arose after them who did not know the LORD nor the work which He had done for Israel.

Israel's Unfaithfulness

[11] Then the children of Israel did evil in the sight of the LORD, and served the Baals; [12] and they forsook the LORD God of their fathers,

who had brought them out of the land of Egypt; and they followed other gods from among the gods of the people who were all around them, and they bowed down to them; and they provoked the LORD to anger. [13] They forsook the LORD and served Baal and the Ashtoreths.

b) You would think, after all God had done for them, the Israelites would eager to obey Him. But what did they do?

They forsook the Lord God of their fathers, which brought them out of the land of Egypt, and followed other gods, of the gods of the people that were round about them, and bowed themselves unto them, and provoked the Lord to anger.

It seems strange that anyone would want to trade a personal, real, living God for a false god that is the figment of man's imagination. But the Canaanite idol Baal was an attractive rival to Yahweh because he was thought to be the god over the weather and nature for the Canaanites; he was essentially the god of agricultural success. In an agricultural society people served Baal because they wanted good weather for abundant crops and flocks.

2. What did Samuel learn about the importance of obedience?

(1 Samuel 15:22): And Samuel said, Hath the Lord as great delight in burnt offerings and sacrifices, as in obeying the voice of the Lord? Behold, to obey is better than sacrifice, and to hearken than the fat of rams.

There are several reasons why obedience to God is better than making sacrifices or offerings to Him:

1. Disobedience is an act of rebellion.
2. Disobedience is sinful.
3. Disobedience is a form of idolatry.
4. Disobedience disrespects God's Word.
5. Disobedience is often based on looking good to other people rather than to God.

3. The best sacrificial offering we could bring to God is ...:

a) Psalm 51:17: The sacrifices of God are a broken spirit:

b) Psalm 51:17: a broken and a contrite heart, O God, thou wilt not despise.

c) Romans 12:1: I beseech you therefore, brethren, by the mercies of God, that ye present your bodies a living sacrifice, holy, acceptable unto God, which is your reasonable service.

Paul used sacrificial language to describe our walk with God. Normally we would think of a sacrifice that would die, but here the idea is that the sacrifice would live. Many people offered sacrifices that would die on the altar, but the Christian is to offer himself or herself as an ongoing sacrifice. By presenting ourselves to God, we become the active agent of God's will.

4. If it were possible to be perfectly obedient to God's laws today, would our obedience gain our entrance into heaven? How do these verses answer that question?

a) Galatians 2:16: Knowing that a man is not justified by the works of the law, but by the faith of Jesus Christ, even we have believed in Jesus Christ, that we might be justified by the faith of Christ, and not by the works of the law: for by the works of the law shall no flesh be justified.

b) Philippians 3:9: And be found in him, not having mine own righteousness, which is of the law, but that which is through the faith of Christ, the righteousness which is of God by faith:

People love to invent their own terms for salvation. They spin their own private schemes of salvation. Some are so satisfied with their own righteousness that they completely overlook God's righteousness by grace. Acceptance of God's grace requires the humility of submission to God's plan of salvation, not our own.

c) Romans 10:3: For they being ignorant of God's righteousness, and going about to establish their own righteousness, have not submitted themselves unto the righteousness of God.

Jews sought to establish their righteousness by human effort, whereas God had already established it for them. They "set up" or erected a righteousness of their own, not God's righteousness. Whenever people set up their own standard for coming to God, they will always miss the target of eternal salvation.

d) Ephesians 2:8-9: 8 For by grace are ye saved through faith; and that not of yourselves: it is the gift of God: 9 Not of works, lest any man should boast.

5. If salvation isn't our reward for obedience, why bother to obey God's or man's laws? When the Apostle Paul was saved, God rewired his heart so that he felt compelled to obey. What was his motivation?

(2 Corinthians 5:14): For the love of Christ constraineth us; because we thus judge, that if one died for all, then were all dead:

6. What makes it possible for us to turn from a life of disobedience and become obedient to God?

(2 Corinthians 5:17; John 14:15): If we are in Christ, we are new creature: old things are passed away; behold, all things are become new.

Let me share testimony of one of my friends about a new creation in Christ she had to the privilege to work with. When she "Linda" and her husband and had their restaurant, there was an employee whom they really loved - but they had to fire him several times for missing work or showing up totally drunk. FINALLY, when they fired him for the 5th time, Mike "the husband of my friend" sat down on the front steps of the restaurant with Billy and shared the gospel message (again). He told him how much we love him and how much Jesus loves him. But they couldn't have him around other employees or the customers when he couldn't even stand up. Billy was about 34 at the time, but didn't even own a car. Mike's heart broke as he watched Billy leave that last time - shuffling home alone in the dark on foot.

About two years later, Billy called and said, "Do you remember me?" Are you kidding? Of course, we had been wondering where he was. Well, Billy said he had just gotten out of prison for drug and alcohol use, and was in a program at a half-way house in Houston. He said that he had met Jesus in prison and wanted to know if we would hire him again. My friend "Linda" told him when he was finished with the program to come see us. Now, sometimes prison conversions aren't real and there is no real fruit - so I was thinking Billy probably just said what he thought we wanted to hear.

About six months later, Billy walked into the restaurant. Mike sat down with him and visited, and decided to offer him a job again. But the only job we had available was for a waiter. Oh. My. No hiding him in the kitchen this time. We contacted DETCOG (the Deep East Texas Council of Government), and told them we wanted to offer Billy a job, but that we only had a waiter position open and his teeth were in too bad of a condition to have him serving food to our guests. The agency said if we would hire him, they would pay for fixing his teeth, and that process actually took over a year.

In the meantime, Billy started serving the customers. Linda took all the orders at a walk-up counter, but he would rush to the register to greet our guests and help them find a table. He was always smiling, always up, always sober. By this time, our customers were saying, "Is that ol' Billy Harper?" Linda don't even recognize him! Last time Linda saw him, he was filthy, knocking on my door at midnight, asking for money." Linda would just smile and say, "Yes, that is Billy. He's a new creation in Christ now." When we sold our restaurant, Billy got a job driving a cement truck - and was very proud of his new position. They went to see him on his job site one more time when we went back for a visit, and he was still smiling from ear to ear. He married a lady with children, so he took on those responsibilities as well. God is good.

7. The right way to live, to experience the abundant life that Jesus talked about, is to ...:

a) Psalm 119:1-4: Blessed are the undefiled in the way, who walk in the law of the Lord. 2 Blessed are they that keep his testimonies, and that seek him with the whole heart. 3 They also do no iniquity: they walk in his ways. 4 Thou hast commanded us to keep thy precepts diligently.

b) John 15:10-11: 10 If ye keep my commandments, ye shall abide in my love; even as I have kept my Father's commandments, and abide in his love.

c) Matthew 6:33: But seek ye first the kingdom of God, and his righteousness; and all these things shall be added unto you.
This must be the rule of our life when ordering our priorities.

8. How would you counsel a person operating under the "I Won't" thinking error?

Pray for God's guidance first, use the Bible and inform the person that to obey the government, for God is the One who has put it there. There is no government anywhere that God has not placed in power.

CHAPTER 15

I DON'T GET
MAD. I GET EVEN

"I Don't Get Mad. I Get Even."

This thinking error actually doesn't make sense, because the only reason a person would decide to get even is if they got mad. But with this mentality, people focus on their anger instead of finding a solution for the problem that set them off. They try to avenge themselves by retaliating in kind, to the same degree as what happened to them. In other words, they find something they can do to the other person that will anger or hurt that person just as much as they have been angered or hurt. If they decide to extract retribution in a violent manner, when they destroy property or harm the other person, they will keep that person focused on their anger too, instead of the real issue.

People who are more vengeful tend to be motivated by power, by authority and by the desire for status. They will say "I don't get mad; I get even," to intimidate others. It's an enforcement technique employed to guarantee cooperation. The intimidator always "wears the pants" in the relationship. Intimidation through any kind of threat is to teach others that they don't matter and their needs don't matter. The intimidator lays down the law and expects you do whatever they want. If you don't, you should expect to suffer the consequences.

The threat of revenge may also serve as a form of self-protection, to make sure others don't get to them first. But the fact is, people who try to control others through vengeful acts are usually out of control themselves. Back and forth retribution, attack and counterattack, getting trapped in a circle of retaliation can destroy the lives of all involved, both from a personal and a legal standpoint.

If you ask someone why they are seeking revenge, they're likely to tell you their goal is catharsis. But instead of giving satisfaction and closure to the person(s) who "got even", revenge actually keeps the wound open and fresh.

Getting even isn't a legal or moral issue as much as it is a spiritual issue. The uniqueness of Christianity should stand out in the way we treat our enemies. But sad to say, even in the church, the vigilante spirit is still alive and well. Christians sometimes attempt to sanctify their anger and urge to get even by calling it righteous indignation, and we have all been tempted to retaliate against those who mistreat us. Paul's teaching about this in Romans 12:17-21 is not popular, because it runs contrary to the inclinations of our flesh.

However, remember that God's thoughts are above ours and His ways are above ours. It is only by His strength that we can live as He requires. With God's mind-set, instead of seeking revenge, we will do good to our enemies, looking for the most practical ways we can help them.

1. What does the Lord say about using revenge to settle a matter?

a) Romans 12:19: "Obey the government, for God is the One who has put it there. There is no government anywhere that God has not placed in power.

Believers are not to pursue retribution against others who have wronged them. It is not our business to exact justice.

b) Matthew 5:38-39: 38 Ye have heard that it hath been said, An eye for an eye, and a tooth for a tooth: 39 But I say unto you, That ye resist not evil: but whosoever shall smite thee on thy right cheek, turn to him the other also.

c) Ephesians 4:26-27: 26 Be ye angry, and sin not: let not the sun go down upon your wrath: 27 Neither give place to the devil.

d) Leviticus 19:18: Thou shalt not avenge, nor bear any grudge against the children of thy people, but thou shalt love thy neighbor as thyself: I am the Lord.

e) Ezekiel 25:17: And I will execute great vengeance upon them with furious rebukes; and they shall know that I am the Lord, when I shall lay my vengeance upon them.

The prerogative of revenge is God's because He knows all the facts. We place the fate of our opponents in the hands of God. He will deal with a situation as it truly is. We do not take the law into our own hands. Redress of a problem could easily come out of personal resentment and not the facts in the case.

f) Hebrews 10:30: For we know him that hath said, Vengeance belongeth unto me, I will recompense, saith the Lord. And again, The Lord shall judge his people.

g) 1 Peter 3:9: Not rendering evil for evil, or railing for railing: but contrariwise blessing; knowing that ye are thereunto called, that ye should inherit a blessing.

h) Proverbs 24:29: Say not, I will do so to him as he hath done to me: I will render to the man according to his work.

Following the principle of this verse is especially difficult when we are under personal attack. In this context we must view God's action against our enemies as something legitimate and our vengeance as finite. We do not have enough information as finite creatures to execute full justice.

i) 1 Thessalonians 5:15: See that none render evil for evil unto any man; but ever follow that which is good, both among yourselves, and to all men.

Revenge has a tendency to boomerang - come back on ourselves. The person who holds on to anger hurts himself in the longer run. We can nurse a grudge until it becomes a full-blown resentment. A biblical Christian repudiates revenge and deliberately accepts undeserved suffering. No one ever truly forgives another person without accepting a loss or a penalty.

2. What does Luke 6:27-28 tell us to do when people have hurt us?

Luke 6:27-28

Love Your Enemies

[27] "But I say to you who hear: Love your enemies, do good to those who hate you, [28] bless those who curse you, and pray for those who spitefully use you.

a): Love your enemies,

b): do good to them which hate you,

c): Bless them that curse you,

d): and pray for them which despitefully use you.

This is a shockingly simple command to understand, but difficult one to obey. And Jesus told us exactly how to manage to carry this out … do good, bless, and pray for them.

3. Luke 6:35 goes even further, and says …: But love ye your enemies, and do good, and lend, hoping for nothing again; and your reward shall be great, and ye shall be the children of the Highest: for he is kind unto the unthankful and to the evil.

If you love people who already love you, what have you accomplished? It's easy to return the love of others and help them out financially. But to love our enemies, and help them with our finances in a time of need is to display the character of Jesus.

4. Instead of getting even, what should we be doing?
(Mark 11:25): And when ye stand praying, forgive, if ye have fought against any: that your Father also which is in heaven may forgive you your trespasses.

5. What will be the result if we show mercy to someone who has hurt us?

(Matthew 5:7): Blessed are the merciful: for they shall obtain mercy.

6. Many people have ruined their health and their lives by hanging on to the poison of bitterness, resentment and unforgiveness, and plotting revenge. Read these scriptures, and tell who in the Bible gave us great examples of forgiving their enemies, and what had been done to them?

a) Genesis 33: Esau.

b) Genesis 50: Joseph

We can't see the big picture as events unfold in our lives. But God has a plan, and it's a plan for success, not failure (Jeremiah 29:11). He will make all events work out for our good in the long run (Romans 8:28).

c) Luke 15: Jesus

d) Luke 23:34: Jesus

e) Acts 7:59-60: Stephen

God answered Stephen's prayer, and used it to touch the heart of a man who actually agreed with the stoning – even though neither Stephen nor the man knew his prayer was being answered. When we get to heaven, we should thank Stephen for every blessing brought through the ministry of Saul of Tarsus, the Apostle Paul.

7. If there is revenge on our minds and unforgiveness in our hearts when we start to pray, what should we do first?
a) Matthew 6:14-15, Mark 11:25-26: to forgive men their trespasses
b) Matthew 5:23-24: First be reconciled to our brothers

In these verses, Jesus is saying that personal, answered prayer is conditioned upon your relationships with others as well as with God. But that's not the way we like it. We want to get what we want from God at the same time as we're snubbing people or are angry and bitter with them. But Jesus warned us that it doesn't work that way.

8. How would you counsel a person operating under the "I don't get mad. I get even" thinking error?

Pray first for God's intervention in the life of the individual you are going to counsel. Try to make the individual understand that anger and revenge can cause more harm that him/her to correct the situation in a civil way as Apostle Paul exhibited in Romans 12:17-21

In this chapter we focused on the spiritual error, but there is also the practical. When you hang on to your anger and talk about your plans for revenge, it can be exhausting for everyone involved. Your friends will get tired of hearing about it. You'll miss out on the joys of life right under your nose. And many have suffered the negative effects on ongoing resentment and bitterness in their health.

CHAPTER 16

MAN ... THIS IS A DRAG

"Man ... This Is a Drag."

Criminals are not interested in doing responsible tasks that don't offer immediate excitement. They find going to work, going to school, going to church a drag. The entire concept of being responsible is mind-numbing to them. If they do become interested in a worthwhile project, their interest is short-lived - unless there is a chance, they'll gain recognition from others by completing it. Most of the time, you'll hear them say things like ... "It's dullsville around here. Color me gone!" Or ... "Man! This job is a drag. I'd rather lay back and just sell some dope." Or ... "These classes are too much work and totally boring. I'm dropping out." Because they can't focus on and stay connected with a task for any length of time and thus can't hold down a job, they may turn to crime to meet their financial needs.

Over the past number of years, I honestly cannot count the number of times that I have seen someone begging for money. There he is, standing with a sign on the side of a busy intersection in big cities as well as small towns. And people saying they only need some changes have approached me in shopping mall parking lots. I don't know if it is just me or if you feel this way, but I am leery of tossing money in the hands of strangers. I always wonder if they can stand on the corner and beg, why can't they spend the same number of hours on a job. Everywhere I go, there are "Help Wanted" signs.

Now we all have friends who are disabled, and would trade their disabilities in a heartbeat for the opportunity to go to work and make a living for their families. That's not who this is about. And there are some who are legitimately down and out, who have "fallen on hard times," who have lost their jobs through downsizing or some other unexpected disaster. It's up to us in the body of Christ to help people through such tough times.

This lesson is about people who find going to work a drag, and so turn instead to crime or begging. Not being willing to accept responsibility and work for a living has as much to do with our spiritual condition as it does our secular mindset. As we read the scriptures for this lesson, we will see God is quite adamant that each of us has a responsibility to do our best to hold down a job, and provide for our family and ourselves to the best of our ability.

1. First, let's see what God says about people who won't work.:

a) 2 Thessalonians 3:10: For even when we were with you, this we commanded you, that if any would not work, neither should he eat.

The Greek emphasizes the phrase "<u>will not</u>." The issue is their obstinate attitude toward the subject of working for food. Laziness goes against many biblical principles. The question here is not refusing to give aid to those who cannot help themselves. He is not talking about people who cannot find a job or people who do not have the physical ability to work. The problem is people with capacity and opportunity to work live exclusively off the graciousness of other people.

The rationale some Thessalonians gave for not working was that Paul taught the imminent return of Christ and that He might come back momentarily. When they ran out of financial resources, they started sponging off their fellow Christians causing relational problems in the church.

b) Proverbs 21:25: The desire of the slothful killeth him; for his hands refuse to labour.

What is worse than being lazy? Being lazy and wanting things! This proverb is closely connected to the next one, "He coveteth greedily all the day long: but the righteous giveth and spareth not" (Proverbs 21:26). It must be frustrating to see things advertised, but love sleep, leisure, sports, and the Internet so much to refuse the needed work, so you end up having nothing (Proverbs 13:4).

c) Proverbs 18:9: He also that is slothful in his work is brother to him that is a great waster.

d) Proverbs 10:4: He becometh poor that dealeth with a slack hand: but the hand of the diligent maketh rich.

e) Proverbs 14:23: In all labour there is profit: but the talk of the lips tendeth only to penury.

Lazy Christians seldom bear fruit or gain a return on God's grace given to them (Luke 8:11-12; 13:6-9; 19:23-27). They squander the opportunity to know God and please Him with their lives. Wasteful Christians hear the word and rejoice and may be active, but they waste their lives chasing the world (Luke 18:14; Philippians 3:18-19; I Timothy 6:6-10).

On the other hand, the Apostle Paul served Jesus with all his might, and he did not waste a single day playing like others (1 Corinthians 15:10; 2 Timothy 4:7). We should follow his example.

2. Instead God says we are to give an honest day's work for an honest day's pay. Paraphrase these verses in your own words.:

a) Ecclesiastes 9:10: We should work as we are alive for in death, where you are going, there is no working or planning, etc.

b) 1 Thessalonians 4:11: People should do all they can to live a peaceful life and should mind their own business, and earn their own living

Christians should mind their own business. A busybody mentality is not of Christ. Many people are much better at telling others how to run their business than at running their own. Personal industry will save busybodies from themselves.

c) Ephesians 4:28: People who are thieves must stop stealing, inter-alia, they should work hard. These people should do something good with their hands so that they'll have something for themself and to share with those in need.

d) 1 Corinthians 15:58: Accordingly, my beloved brethren, become stedfast, unmovable, abounding in the work of the Lord at all times, knowing that your labour is not vain in the Lord.

There are two kinds of people in ministry: (1) those willing to minister, and (2) those willing to let others minister. The church today stands in dire need for workers, yet there is little passion for ministry because most people have lost their sense of conviction. No excuse will be an adequate rationalization before God at the Judgment Seat of Christ.

3. What are some other dangers of not working?

a) 2 Thessalonians 3:11-12: For we hear that there are some who walk among you in a disorderly manner, not working at all, but are busybodies. 12 Now those who are such we command and exhort through our Lord Jesus Christ that they work in quietness and eat their own bread.

b) 1 Timothy 5:8-9: 8 But if anyone does not provide for his own, and especially for those of his household, he has denied the faith and is worse than an unbeliever. 9 Do not let a widow under sixty years old be taken into the number, and not unless she has been the wife of one man,

4. What is to be our attitude when working?

a) 1 Corinthians 10:31: do all to the glory of God.

We should work as hard as if Jesus were our boss. Or, we should work as hard as if Jesus were our customer. We should do our best at all times, so that the work of our hands glorifies God and is a testimony to others who are watching us.

b) Colossians 3:23-24: 23 And whatever you do, do it heartily, as to the Lord and not to men, 24 knowing that from the Lord you will receive the reward of the inheritance; for you serve the Lord Christ.

5. How would you counsel a person operating under the "Man ... this is a drag" thinking error?

First pray the talk to the individual, try to let him know that nothing comes easy and nothing is easy and the best things are the hardest. I will Quote — Theodore Roosevelt: "Nothing in the world is worth having or worth doing unless it means effort, pain, difficulty… I have never in my life envied a human being who led an easy life. I have envied a great many people who led difficult lives and led them well."

Today many slackers have the entitlement mentality — especially if their parents lived off of welfare benefits. But believers must be diligent and hard workers, both with regard to heavenly and on earthly duties, and in that order with a clear priority. They must follow the example of Jesus, Who said, "I must work the works of Him that sent me, while it is day: the night cometh, when no man can work" (John 9:4).

CHAPTER 17

THAT IS NONE OF YOUR BUSINESS

"That's None of Your Business."

Individuals with this thinking error are good at pointing out others' problems, giving feedback on the faults of others, but want you to mind your own business when it comes to your offering advice on their own issues. When everyone else is talking about personal subjects, they will typically hang back and not contribute, change the subject, give vague or evasive answers, or decide this is a good time to get up and leave.

They're usually a little on edge in a group, because they don't know when the attention might turn to them, and uncomfortable questions arise. They become touchy and defensive when people try to ask about their lives. They even clam up when asked for details about themselves that most people would share freely with anyone – like what kind of movies they like, or what they did or where they were last week. This tendency to keep things close to the chest may have started in childhood, when they got proficient at covering up family problems such as an alcoholic father or physical abuse, and it just became second nature by adulthood.

Such a person also lies by omission; they don't give you the full story. For example, they might defend themselves by saying, "I didn't lie. I said I wasn't at work on Friday. I just didn't tell you I was fired for being late again." Or you might hear, "That's stupid. You don't know what you're talking about. "But they decline to give you the rest of the information you need to make an informed judgment about a situation.

Such people are usually also emotionally closed off, and don't allow themselves to be affected by your needs or desires. If fact, they may be downright cold and unfeeling. They can be emotionally abusive, manipulative, controlling, and passive-aggressive.

Erecting a protective shell about themselves, and keeping their personal plans private, are elements of the secretive nature of a criminal. If you simply accept it as an integral part of their personality, it gives them the freedom to do as they wish without argument.

One spiritual issue with this character trait is that they may also have closed themselves off from God and the saving grace of Jesus Christ. They are unable to allow themselves to be transparent with God about their sins, or draw close to Him. They have never experienced "the peace that passes all understanding." Scripture doesn't comfort them, and your prayers bore them. But they know something is missing.

I believe the older brother of the prodigal son was somewhat like this. He wasn't a criminal – he stayed home and did everything his father asked. But I find it strange that he was all by himself during the first part of the story.

1. Read Luke 15.:

a) What was the older son doing when his younger brother returned home? He was in the field.

b) What did he hear when he came home at the end of the day, tired and dusty? And as he came and drew near to the house, he heard music and dancing.

c) Why did his father come out to speak to him in verse 28? He was angry and would not go in.

The older son was outraged that his father was throwing a party for his wild younger brother. But the truth is, he probably thought about doing same things when he was young, but was either too scared or never had the opportunity to do them. In this scenario, he was guilty of judging both his father and his brother.

d) Do the scriptures let us know if the older son attended the party, after his father spoke to him about it? No

e) On what was the older son's focus fixed? Was on the possession his father had. He was waiting for his father, may be to die so that he can inherit the wealth.

The son said, "I never transgressed … you never gave." These exaggerations are common for people who hold on to bitterness. The older son finally showed this bitterness to the father, but only after it had done its damage in his heart over many years. Proud and self-righteous people always feel that they are not being treated as well as they deserve.

f) On what is the closed-off person's mind fixed? On the things and their own desires.

g) To correct this thinking error, on what should the closed-off, "mind your own business" type of person focus? They should focus on God and the saving grace of Jesus Christ.

That is a possible answer. I was thinking we should shift our focus to others, on what they need or how they are feeling. But this is not the way the world thinks. They think we should be egocentric, looking out for #1, putting our own wellbeing ahead of others. But people who put themselves first are seldom happy. Instead, the Bible tells us that we should:

1. Put Jesus first. Give Him the pre-eminence or first place in everything (Matthew 6:33, Colossians 1:18).
2. Put others second. Make sacrifices for others, humbly putting their needs ahead of your own (Philippians 2:3).
3. Put yourself last. This was the attitude of Christ, who emptied Himself taking on the form of a servant (Matthew 20:16, 27-28).

2. David knew how it was to feel distant from God and others. He probably would have related to the older brother. Share some of what he was feeling in these verses.:

a) Psalm 13:1: How long, O Lord? Will You forget me forever? How long will You hide Your face from me?

b) Psalm 22:1: My God, My God, why have You forsaken Me? Why are You so far from helping Me, And from the words of My groaning?

One of the things I love about the Psalms is the honesty of David. He pours his heart out. Even though he felt that God had abandoned him, he prayed. Even in despair, he still prayed. Even in the lowest moments of his life, he reached out to God. He always took his frustration and laid it at the feet of his God. He never quit praying.

But one of the things that David often did in times of despair was to remember. You will find him worshipping and you will also find him telling stories of how God moved in his life in the past. You see, in low moments we often think that this is the worst we've ever had it. But, if you will stop and think and remember - God will help you to see times where he has come to your rescue before.

My favorite song right now is "<u>Do It Again</u>." If you are feeling discouraged about anything, stop and listen to this song.

3. Jesus experienced this when He said ... (Matthew 27:46): And about the ninth hour Jesus cried out with a loud voice, saying, "Eli, Eli, lama sabachthani? "that is, "My God, My God, why have You forsaken Me?"

Jesus had known great pain and suffering (both physical and emotional) during His life. But He had never known separation from His Father. At this moment, He experienced what He had not yet ever experienced. There was a significant sense in which Jesus rightly felt forsaken by the Father at this moment.

4. Meet with God first thing in the morning, and talk to Him about your plans for the day (pray). Name some heroes in the Bible who spent time alone with God in prayer.:

a) Genesis 21:33: Then Abraham planted a tamarisk tree in Beersheba, and there called on the name of the Lord, the Everlasting God.

b) Genesis 24:63: And Isaac went out to meditate in the field in the evening; and he lifted his eyes and looked, and there, the camels were coming.

c) Exodus 24:14-15: 14 Now let it be that the young woman to whom I say, 'Please let down your pitcher that I may drink,' and she says, 'Drink, and I will also give your camels a drink'—let her be the one You have appointed for Your servant Isaac. And by this I will know that You have shown kindness to my master." 15 And it happened, before he had finished speaking, that behold, Rebekah, who was born to Bethuel, son of Milcah, the wife of Nahor, Abraham's brother, came out with her pitcher on her shoulder.

d) 1 Samuel 1:9-13: 9 So Hannah arose after they had finished eating and drinking in Shiloh. Now Eli the priest was sitting on the seat by the doorpost of the tabernacle of the Lord. 10 And she was in bitterness of soul, and prayed to the Lord and [b]wept in anguish. 11 Then she made a vow and said, "O Lord of hosts, if You will indeed look on the affliction of Your maidservant and remember me, and not forget Your maidservant, but will give Your maidservant a male child, then I will give him to the Lord all the days of his life, and no razor shall come upon his head." 12 And it happened, as she continued praying before the Lord, that Eli watched her mouth. 13 Now Hannah spoke in her heart; only her lips moved, but her voice was not heard. Therefore, Eli thought she was drunk.

e) Daniel 6:10: Now when Daniel knew that the writing was signed, he went home. And in his upper room, with his windows open toward Jerusalem, he knelt down on his knees three times that day, and prayed and gave thanks before his God, as was his custom since early days.

Daniel had a habit and place of prayer. He allowed nothing to interfere with this practice. He was a man who utterly depended on God for his needs. Guidance and thanksgiving were part of his prayer life. The words "as was his custom since early days" tells us that it his customary practice from the beginning of his walk with God.

f) Mark 6:46: And when He had sent them away, He departed to the mountain to pray.

g) Acts 10:9: The next day, as they went on their journey and drew near the city, Peter went up on the housetop to pray, about the sixth hour.

5. Get into God's Word every day.:

a) We need nourishment from God's Word to grow. "Man shall not live by bread alone, but by ... (Matthew 4:4): every word that proceeds from the mouth of God.

Jesus could have stood against Satan with a display of His own glory. He could have stood against Satan with logic and reason. Instead, Jesus used the word of God as a weapon against Satan and temptation.

b) If we draw near God in His Word, He will ... (James 4:8): He will draw near to you. Cleanse your hands, you sinners; and purify your hearts, you double-minded.

When we draw near to God, God will draw near to us. But God requires that we exercise our volition toward Him first. God will embrace any believer no matter how long or to what extent he went away from Him. God stands ready to accept us with open arms. Psalm 145:18 says, "The Lord is near to all who call upon Him, to all who call upon Him in truth."

c) The Word is our best defense against ... (Ephesians 6:13): the evil day, and having done all, to stand.

d) Faith comes by hearing, and hearing by ... (Romans 10:17): the word of God.

Faith in Jesus doesn't come by some mystical experience, or any method other than spoken words. Trust in what God says comes from hearing the gospel. Belief will come to people who are open to hearing the truth. That it is why it is such an important responsibility to talk to people about Jesus and the way to salvation.

e) We need to be corrected when we sin. Job 6:24 says ...: "Teach me, and I will hold my tongue; Cause me to understand wherein I have erred.

6. Just mediate. God speaks about meditation in several places throughout the Bible, encouraging us to get quiet, and just think about His Word. Our thoughts determine our behavior, and so what we think about is very important.:

a) When are we to meditate? (Psalm 1:2): But his delight is in the law of the Lord, And in His law he meditates day and night

b) On what are we to mediate? (Joshua 1:8): This Book of the Law shall not depart from your mouth, but you shall meditate in it day and night, that you may observe to do according to all that is written in it. For then you will make your way prosperous, and then you will have good success.

c) What are we to be thinking about while we are meditating? (Philippians 4:8): Finally, brethren, whatever things are true, whatever things are noble, whatever things are just, whatever things are pure, whatever things are lovely, whatever things are of good report, if there is any virtue and if there is anything praiseworthy— meditate on these things.

God wants us to replace our way of thinking with His way of thinking so our actions line up with God's viewpoint. In this verse we find a catalog of thinking for developing a proper mental attitude.

d) What are some benefits of meditating on God's Word? (Jeremiah 31:33): But this is the covenant that I will make with the house of Israel after those days, says the Lord: I will put My law in their minds, and write it on their [a]hearts; and I will be their God, and they shall be My people.

God can change the minds and hearts of those who are connected to Him through His Word.

7. Would might you suggest as a first step to someone who is completely closed off, operating under the "That's None of Your Business" thinking error?

Let them be emotionally not closed off, and allow themselves to be affected by their needs or desires.

CHAPTER 18

I WANT IT NOW

"I Want It NOW!"

This thinking error related to this statement is referred to as "lack of time perspective." A criminal often demands immediate possession of what he wants. He interprets "wants" as needs, and refuses to wait and work for them. Criminals with this thinking error will often decide to go ahead and take by stealth or force what they want, especially if they don't have the cash on hand to buy it.

Another thinking error to which this statement relates is "materialism." This is the tendency to consider material possessions and physical comfort as more important than spiritual or moral values. The law has no impact on their thinking when they decide to go ahead and acquire something they want.

Sometimes people with the "I want it now" thinking error turn to shoplifting. They basically say to themselves, "If I can take it, I will take it." For many, it's an irresistible urge. There's something in their brain telling them, "You want it, right? So go ahead and take it." Shoplifting can become a genuine addiction that stems from the same issue as a gambling or drinking addiction. These people shoplift because they feel compelled to, rather than for financial or material gain.

We shouldn't point an accusing finger at these people. Wanting what we want right now, rather than waiting for it, may have gotten some of us in trouble with our credit cards. The reality of high credit card debt for many people is that they spent money they didn't have and don't have a way to pay back. They max out their credit line to have what they want right now. Thinking that $2,000 flat-screen TV only costs $20 per month in payments is dangerous, and can quickly lead to overwhelming debt.

Debt is an unwelcome guest in the home of many Americans. The average U.S. household with debt carries $15,310 in credit card debt and $132,086 in total debt (auto loan, house mortgage, and credit card combined). The average number of credit cards owned by each adult American is 3.7. According to 2015 statistics, the average household is paying a total of $6,658 in interest per year. This is 9% of the average household income ($75,591) being spent on interest alone.

I see at least spiritual issues with this thinking error. One is failure to recognize that God is our generous Provider. We don't have to go out and get everything ourselves. He will give it to us when the time is right. Which brings us to the second spiritual issue … failure to wait on God. Let's examine both in the Word.

1. Read Genesis 22.:

a) What instructions did God give Abraham to test his obedience?

God said to Abraham, Take now thy son, thine only son Isaac, whom thou lovest, and get thee into the land of Moriah; and offer him there for a burnt offering upon one of the mountains which I will tell thee of.

Abraham had obeyed God many times in his walk with Him, but no test could have been more severe than the one in Genesis 22. This was an astounding command because Isaac was the son of promise. God had promised several times that from Abraham's own body would come a nation as multitudinous as the stars in heaven (Genesis 12:2–3; 15:4–5). Later, Abraham was specifically told that the promise would be through Isaac (Genesis 21:12).

b) After a three-day journey, Abraham took his son to the top of a mountain to carry out this act of obedience. What was the name of the mountain? Mount Moriah

c) When Isaac asked where the sacrifice was, how did Abraham answer? Abraham said, My son, God will provide himself a lamb for a burnt offering:

d) Abraham was completely willing to plunge the knife into Isaac, because of his faith. But when Abraham displayed his obedient heart towards God, what did God do? And the angel of the Lord called unto him out of heaven, and said, Abraham, Abraham: and he said, Here am I. 12 And he said, Lay not thine hand upon the lad, neither do thou anything unto him: for now I know that thou fearest God, seeing thou hast not withheld thy son, thine only son from me.

I think Abraham's faith was so deep that, even if he had plunged the knife and sacrificed Isaac, he believed the Lord would keep His word and raise Isaac from the dead (Hebrews 11:17–19). God uses Abraham's faith as an example of the type of faith required for salvation. Genesis 15:6 says, "Abram believed the LORD, and he credited it to him as righteousness."

e) What did Abraham call the name of that place from then on? Jehovah Jireh

2. What are some of the ways God provides mentioned in Psalm 65:9-13.:

a): The grain

b): bless its growth.

c): paths drip with abundance.

d): Flocks

There are at least 169 verses in the Bible that refer to the ways God provides for us. Philippians 4:19 puts it simply: "My God will supply all your needs according to His riches in glory in Christ Jesus."

3. In Matthew 6:26, Jesus told the people to look at how birds are provided for by God. If He takes care of even the birds, we should expect that ...: God will provide our need. Exhibit: Look at the birds of the air, for they neither sow nor reap nor gather into barns; yet your heavenly Father feeds them. Are you not of more value than they?

This section of the Sermon on the Mount gives seven arguments against worry:

1. If God gave life, He will sustain life (Matthew 6:25).
2. It is God's nature to supply for His creatures (Matthew 6:26).
3. Worry is useless (Matthew 6:27).
4. Man as the crown of creation shows the futility of worry (Matthew 6:28-31).
5. Worry is characteristic of unbelievers (Matthew 6:32a).
6. God's providential care shows there is no need for worry (Matthew 6:32b-33).
7. Worry for more than what is at hand compounds worry (Matthew 6:34).

4. In Luke 9:11-17, we see that Jesus doesn't just care about our spiritual needs. He also has a real concern for our physical and material needs as well.:

a) How many loaves and fishes did the disciples have to feed the 5000? five loaves and two fish

b) How many basketfuls did the disciples gather after the crowd was fed? twelve baskets of the leftover fragments were taken up by them.

We see a similar example in 2 Kings 4:42-44. Elijah fed one hundred men with some barley loaves and ears of grain – with some left over.

c) Why did Jesus use the boy's lunch to feed the people? Why didn't he create their lunch from nothing? (Thought question – answers will vary.): Jesus was showing His disciples that to God all things are possible.

I think the lesson is that our duty is to yield all we have to Him, and then to obey Him when He tells us what to do with it.

5. To wait on the Lord is to trust Him completely with our lives. It means looking to Him as the way, the truth, and the life. He is our source.:

a) Waiting is not a virtue at which most of us excel. What is promised to those who wait upon the Lord? (Isaiah 40:31): But those who wait on the Lord, Shall renew their strength; They shall mount up with wings like eagles, They shall run and not be weary, They shall walk and not faint.

Prayer and Bible study and meditating upon God's Word are essential when we're waiting. To wait on the Lord we need a heart responsive to the Word of God, with a focus on the things of heaven, and a patience rooted in faith.

b) David knew personally the need to wait upon the Lord.

What character trait did he instruct us to exhibit as we wait? (Psalm 27:14b): Be of good courage,

It's easy to say we trust God, but our response to delays, frustrations, and difficult situations exposes where we are actually placing our hope.

- Are we convinced God is listening?
- Do we believe he's good?
- Do we accept that our circumstances are sovereignly ordained?
- Do we doubt He really cares about us?

When we choose to wait courageously and patiently, we not only honor God but encourage others to put their hope in him as well.

c) What will the Lord do when we courageously wait on Him? (Psalm 27:14c): And He shall strengthen your heart;

6. The advice to wait on the Lord is a recurring theme in the book of Psalms. What are some of the benefits of waiting on the Lord, instead of charging ahead and taking care of things ourselves?

a) Psalm 25:3a: Indeed, let no one who waits on You be ashamed;

b) Psalm 25:21: Let integrity and uprightness preserve me, For I wait for You.

c) Psalm 27:14, 31:24: Wait[a] on the Lord; Be of good courage, And He shall strengthen your heart; Wait, I say, on the Lord! Be of good courage, And He shall strengthen your heart, All you who hope in the Lord.

d) Psalm 33:20: Our soul waits for the Lord; He is our help and our shield.

e) Psalm 37:9, 34: For evildoers shall be cut off: but those that wait upon the LORD, they shall inherit the earth. Wait on the LORD, and keep his way, and he shall exalt thee to inherit the land: when the wicked are cut off, thou shalt see it.

f) Psalm 39:7: "But now, Lord, what do I look for? My hope is in you.

Waiting on the Lord is something the godly do. It's about holding on tight, hoping with expectation and trust, knowing that our Lord is not making us wait just to see how long we can "take it." There are times when God will delay His answer, and we will at times wonder why He seems so reluctant to intervene in our affairs: "I am worn out calling for help; my throat is parched. My eyes fail, looking for my God" (Psalm 69:3). But, knowing the Lord, we trust that He will come at the perfect moment, not a second too soon or too late.

g) Psalm 40:1: For the director of music. Of David. A psalm. I waited patiently for the LORD; he turned to me and heard my cry.

h) Psalm 62:1: For the director of music. For Jeduthun. A psalm of David. Truly my soul finds rest in God; my salvation comes from him.

i) Psalm 104:27: All creatures look to you to give them their food at the proper time.

j) Psalm 106:13: But they soon forgot what he had done and did not wait for his plan to unfold.

When we don't choose to wait on the Lord, we bring trouble down on ourselves. Remember how Abraham and Sarah did not wait on the Lord for their child of promise. Instead, Sarah offered her maid, Hagar, to Abraham in order to have a child through her. Scripture offers plenty of other examples of saints who got weary of waiting for God and chose to do things their way. I've given way to that temptation myself.

God's goodness is promised for those who wait patiently for him! No matter how long. Regardless of how hopeless things appear to us. Even when it seems to cost us everything. "God is able to do far more abundantly than all that we ask or think, according to his power at work within us" (Ephesians 3:20). When we wait for him, we will never be disappointed.

7. What Biblical advice would you give to someone who wants everything RIGHT NOW? To depend on the Lord and King David said: A Psalm of David. The Lord is my shepherd; I shall not want. He makes me lie down in green pastures. He leads me beside still waters. He restores my soul. He leads me in paths of righteousness for his name's sake. Even though I walk through the valley of the shadow of death, I will fear no evil, for you are with me; your rod and your staff, they comfort me. You prepare a table before me in the presence of my enemies; you anoint my head with oil; my cup overflows. ...

I found a list of 10 things to do while you're waiting on God.
1. Believe that the God who saved you hears your cries (Micah 7:7).
2. Watch Watch with expectancy, but be prepared for unexpected answers (Psalm 5:3).
3. Put your hope in his Word (Psalm 130:5-6).
4. Trust in the Lord, not in your own understanding (Proverbs 3:5-6).

5. Resist fretting, refrain from anger, be still, and choose
   patience (Psalm 37:7-8).
6. Be strong and take courage (Psalm 27:13-14; 31:24).
7. See it as an opportunity to experience God's goodness
    (Psalm 27:13; Lamentations 3:25).
8. Wait for God's promise instead of going your own way
    (Acts 1:4).
9. Continue steadfastly in prayer, being watchful with
   thanksgiving (Colossians 4:2).
10. Remember the blessings yet to come (Isaiah 30:18).

CHAPTER 19

I WILL GIT'ER DONE TOMORROW

"I'll Git'er Done Tomorrow"

Another example of this same thinking error, the lack of time perspective, involves the tendency to say, "Why worry about that now? I've got plenty of time." Children demonstrate this thinking error when it comes to weekends and doing their homework. They want to wait until the last minute on Sunday night to get it done. As adults, we might put off paying bills, until they're delinquent. We wait to get caught up until the debt collectors have handed over our bills to collection agents and the pressure to pay has increased.

We see this in criminals when they dilly-dally around, and come up with one excuse after another, to put off doing responsible things – like get a real job. Procrastination is actually fear cloaked in nonchalance. They know that if they never start a job, they'll never have a chance to fail and get fired from the job. But if they don't go for the job, they'll never have a chance to succeed, either.

You will also see this in ex-offenders' lives when they keep putting off meeting with their probation or parole agent, because it could be unpleasant … or it takes time out of their day … or they don't have the money. It is usually a condition of probation or parole that an ex-offender pays for the cost of supervision, or at least a portion of what it costs to supervise a probationer or parolee. My granddaughter ran from the law one time because she didn't have the $50 to pay her parole officer. Finally, an ex-offender will show up at their meeting because it has become a priority; not showing up could mean the loss of their freedom with no more opportunities for parole.

Procrastinators' problems run deep. The more they ignore their responsibilities and keep putting things off to tomorrow, the more they spend their time in a state of urgency, and even panic, trying to address the things that have gotten out of control in their lives. It takes something more than "being more self-disciplined" or "changing bad habits" for the procrastinator to change his/her ways. It takes God.

This thinking error points to an issue of time management beyond how we use our time every day. Ephesians 5:15-16 says, "See then that ye walk circumspectly, not as fools, but as wise, redeeming the time, because the days are evil." Paul isn't just telling us to make the most of every moment in every day, although that is certainly good advice. He is telling us to make the most of the time we have left on earth, because time is running out and we need to share the good news of the Gospel with everyone we can.

1. The older we get, the more we think about using our time wisely in light of eternity. We try to evaluate what really matters. Moses must have been feeling this when he prayed the words recorded in Psalm 90.:

a) How did Moses spend his first 40 years? (Exodus 2:1-15): He grew up in the Kings Palace as the son of Pharaoh's daughter. He was a Prince. He then killed an Egyptian.

b) How did Moses spend his next 40 years? (Exodus 2:11 – 7:7): Moses was in exile.

c) How did Moses spend the final 40 years of his life? (Exodus 7:8-13 to Deuteronomy 34:12): Moses was a prophet of God, he lead the Israelites out of Egypt.

From the palace of Pharaoh, to the desert wilderness of a fugitive shepherd, to the place of service leading the chosen people of God, we can reflect on the life of Moses, and see how God is at work through the different seasons of our own lives. As the psalmist says, "My times are in Your hand" (Psalm 31:15).

2. What are some of the things Jesus accomplished during His 3 short years of ministry? (Thought questions – answers will vary.):

a): He introduced to the humanity to the Kingdom of God

b): He introduced the Father to us.

c): He reconciled man to Himself.

d): He died so that we may live.

Here is a chronological list of everything Jesus did during His 3-1/2 years of ministry. I wonder what our own ministry list would look like.

- Baptism & Anointing
- First 2 following Jesus
- 40 days in wilderness
- 1st miracle (Water to Wine)
- Visit to Capernaum
- Jerusalem visit
- Temple Cleansed (1st time)
- Nicodemus
- Contention between disciples
- 1st withdrawal from Judea
- Woman at the well
- Nobleman's son healed
- Prison for John the Baptist
- First visit to Nazareth
- Healing at the Pool of Bethesda
- Preaching from Peter's Boat
- The "Move" to Capernaum
- Madman healed in Capernaum
- Peter's mother-in-law healed
- First Galilean tour

- Lone leper healed
- Man let down through the roof
- "Harvesting" on the Sabbath
- Withered hand healed
- Matthew called
- The 12 disciples ordained
- Sermon on the Mount (Beatitudes)
- 2nd Galilean tour
- Widow's son of Nain raised to life
- "Who is my mother?"
- Calms the sea
- 2 demoniacs healed
- Blind and mute man healed
- Roman Centurian's servant healed
- John asks about Jesus
- Matthew's feast
- Jairus' daughter
- One touch heals
- 3rd Galilean tour
- Sent two by two
- Rejected at Nazareth again
- John is beheaded
- Retreats to quiet spot
- 5000 fed
- Walks on water
- Many leave Him
- No Jerusalem trip (trap set)
- Canaanite woman's daughter healed
- 4000+ fed
- Blind man healed (Bethsaida)
- The Transfiguration
- Demon possessed boy healed
- Returns to Capernaum
- Argument about who is the greatest
- Tax from fish's mouth
- Visit to Jerusalem in secret
- Teaches in the Temple
- Writes in the dust

- Puts clay on man's eyes
- Returns to Galilee
- Begins last journey to Jerusalem
- 70 appointed
- Visits Mary and Martha
- Lazarus Raised from the dead
- High Priest, "Better one should die...."
- Visits with Zacchaeus
- Rich young ruler
- Blessing of the children
- Heals 10 lepers (1 says thanks)
- Suffers and dies on the Cross
- Resurrected from the dead
- Ascended to heaven 40 day after resurrection

4. The apostle Paul was also a man of godly purpose. He lived to exalt Christ and to know Him. At the end of his life, as he faced execution, Paul knew that he had … (2 Timothy 4:7):

a): fought a good fight,

b): finished his course

c): kept the faith

d): preached the gospel

Throughout his ministry Paul used the picture of the race and the Christian being an athlete running that race (Philippians 3:12-14, Acts 20:24, 1 Corinthians 9:24, Hebrews 12:1). At the time he wrote this letter to Timothy, he knew his race was just about finished.

4. What did Paul know would be his reward, for making every moment count in serving His Lord and Savior? Eternal life with Jesus

There are two main words for crown in the New Testament. One refers to a royal crown and the other to the victor's crown. Here Paul referred to the victor's crown – the crown that was essentially a trophy, recognizing that one had competed according to the rules and had won the victory.

Paul knew there was a crown waiting for him in heaven, and he was ready to receive it. He was certain of it.

5. Read Ephesians 5:16 again, and then read Colossians 4:5.: a) What phrase is the same in both verses? Use your time in the best way you can.

The idea of "redeeming the time" is to buy up opportunities. "Redeeming" means to buy up or buy back. This term was used for buying back a slave after he had been sold. The idea is to make a slave free by a purchase. We are to buy up all the opportunities that come our way.

We have only so much time on earth. Redeemed time implies the value of timely situations. We need to avail ourselves of opportunities that lie before us. We must make every moment count for the Lord. God allots a definite limit of opportunities. We are to seize on those opportunities when the Lord affords them to us.

b) Why did Paul say we are to make the most of every minute? Because these are evil times and we do not know the time or the hour the Savior is coming

Yes. "Time" does not mean the succession of events. The word used here is the word for season or opportunity. We are to seize openings as they occur. There will be times in our lives where opportunities for ministry occur and we need to take advantage of them. There will be limited occasions where there is an open door and we can perhaps lead someone to the Lord.

6. To redeem the time, we must know what God wants us to be and how to get there. What are some ways we can use our time for His glory? (Thought questions – answers will vary.):

a): I should see each day as a gift from God. "My times are in your hands" (Psalm 31:15).

b): To commit my time to God. The Bible says, "Teach us to number our days aright, that we may gain a heart of wisdom" (Psalm 90:12).

c): To set aside time for God and for others. "Seek first his kingdom and his righteousness" (Matthew 6:33)

7. How would you counsel a person who thinks they have all the time in the world, who has problems with time management, who wastes time, and always promises to "git'er done tomorrow:

Pray for God's direction, in the same token, use the Word of God to guide the individual. As Apostle Paul said: Ephesians 5:15-16 says, "See then that ye walk circumspectly, not as fools, but as wise, redeeming the time, because the days are evil." Instead of seeing each day as a burden, see it instead as another opportunity God has given you to serve Him. Time isn't inexhaustible, nor can we assume we'll always have more; someday our time on earth will end.

We may not feel like it, but people today have more free time than ever before. For most of human history, people had to spend almost every waking moment providing food, clothing and shelter for themselves and their families. Actually, it's still that way in much of the world.

But, according to a recent report by the U.S. Department of Labor, Americans over the age of 15 average more than five hours of free time a day. That's almost a third of the time we're awake! And, according to the same report, most of that unprecedented leisure time is used for entertainment - TV, surfing the internet, video games, checking our social media accounts.

God set the first priority for organizing our free time by mandating one day of rest time each week, the Sabbath day, for us to deepen our relationship with Him, with our family and with other Christians. This shows the importance of taking time to reflect on life, to take stock and to verify that we are pursuing what is most important in life.

Then, regarding the rest of our free time, the apostle Peter wrote that we will "give an account" to God for the way we use our lives and what we accomplish (1 Peter 4:3-6). What will we be able to tell God in that accounting? Will we have to tell Him of hours wasted in mindless and destructive entertainment, or will we be able to show character development, spiritual growth and time spent in service to Him and our fellow man?

CHAPTER 20

I WON'T GET CAUGHT

"I Won't Get Caught"

Criminals strategize every move while planning crimes. They envision what will happen from the moment they dream up their escapade until after they make their getaway. They know the occupational hazards of the crime include the possibilities of getting caught, convicted, wounded, or even killed.

By the time a criminal is prepared to carry out his crime, he is certain he will succeed and he has completely eliminated these possibilities of failure from his mind. He is operating under the thinking error known as "super optimism," and regards the crime as not only completed, but completely wrapped up as an unqualified success.

The criminal with the "super optimism" thinking error believes that if he decides he wants to do something, he can consider it as good as done. As he plans his next illegal offense, he lives in a state of absolute certainty that he won't get caught, no matter how ridiculous his plan. He doesn't entertain reasonable doubts about anything he wants done.

His experience supports this certainty. He knows the likelihood of being arrested is low. He previously has gotten away with crimes without anyone suspecting him as the perpetrator. Although he is aware of the possibility that he could slip up, that things can go wrong, he is absolutely certain that it won't happen "this time."

Inmates have come to understand that super optimism is the thinking error that kills criminals more than anything else. As an offender gets away with more and more crimes, he becomes more and more emboldened and develops a sense of invulnerability. He will begin to take greater and greater chances. In some cases, drug usage has contributed to this recklessness. Sometimes criminals who got away with complicated crimes in the past become overconfident and let down their guard, getting caught while committing a relatively minor offense.

If he plans to "one day" become a responsible person, he feels confident he will succeed at that too. He uses super optimism to convince himself that he doesn't really have to work at things to make them turn out all right … he believes things will just fall in place for him without effort. He doesn't see the connection between work and success … whether relating to a job, a relationship with someone he cares about, or staying out of prison upon release.

1. Criminals commonly operate under the thinking error that they won't get caught. But in the Old Testament, God knew people would get caught and decreed the punishment for each crime in advance. What was the penalty for stealing in these verses?

a) Proverbs 6:31: But if he is caught, he must pay back seven times what he stole. It may cost him everything he owns.

This proverb is part actually of Solomon's condemnation of adultery, for there is no way to pay a person back for that crime (Proverbs 6:27-35). We can understand why a person might steal due to hunger, but we will still require full restoration. But adultery cannot be undone by any amount of payment. It violates a man's most intimate possession without any possibility of restoration or replacement.

b) Exodus 22:1: Then he must pay back five bulls for the one bull he stole. Or he must pay back four sheep for the one sheep he stole.

The Mosaic Law did not send a person to jail because of theft. Instead, the thief was required to restore what he stole, plus an additional penalty. The reason for the fivefold penalty in the case of stealing an ox is probably because one man stole the means of another man's livelihood.

2. What was the penalty when someone was caught murdering another?

a) Genesis 9:6: will be killed by a human being.

b) Exodus 21:12: "That night I will go through the land of Egypt. I will kill all the firstborn of animals and people in the land of Egypt. I will punish all the gods of Egypt. I am the Lord.

The principle for capital punishment goes back to Genesis 9:6. The right for the state to use the sword of execution is also stated in the New Testament (Romans 13:3-4).

3. What was required before the sentence for murder could be carried out?

(Numbers 35:30): And there must be witnesses. No one may be put to death with only one witness.

4. What was the penalty when someone was caught in a sexual sin?

a) Leviticus 20:13: They must be put to death. They have brought it on themselves.

b) Deuteronomy 22:20-21: the girl must be brought to the door of her father's house. Then the men of the town must put her to death by throwing stones at her.

c) John 8:4-5: The law of Moses commands that we kill with stones every woman who does this. What do you say we should do?"

According to the Mosaic law, the witnesses were required to be the ones who threw the first stone. So, Jesus was asking for the witnesses to step forward — the witnesses, who were still bound by an oath to tell the truth and nothing but the truth — and cast the first stones. But they couldn't.

By this action, Jesus showed the compassionate heart of God toward sinners and silenced the mob's hypocritical allegations.

5. Is it possible to "get away with murder" here on earth? Yes

6. We may be able to hide our sins (crimes) from man. But what do the following verses say about the possibility of hiding our sins from God?

a) Genesis 3:8-10: 8 Then they heard the Lord God walking in the garden. This was during the cool part of the day. And the man and his wife hid from the Lord God among the trees in the garden. 9 But the Lord God called to the man. The Lord said, "Where are you?" 10 The man answered, "I heard you walking in the garden. I was afraid because I was naked. So, I hid."

b) Jeremiah 16:17: I see everything they do. They cannot hide the things they do from me. Their sin is not hidden from my eyes!

c) Jeremiah 23:24: "No one can hide. where I cannot see him," says the Lord. "I fill all of heaven and earth," says the Lord.

d) Psalm 69:5: "I fill all of heaven and earth," says the Lord. I cannot hide my guilt from you.

e) Hebrews 4:13: Nothing in all the world can be hidden from God. Everything is clear and lies open before him. And to him we must explain the way we have lived.

The original Greek word for "open" here was used to refer to wrestlers who had a hold that involved gripping the neck and was so powerful that it brought victory. There is no one and nothing that is hidden from God. Everything is open to His eyes, and He sees our heart and knows how to reach us.

7. A 20-year study found that 30% of the population will steal, not only if the opportunity arises, but also will create the opportunity whenever possible. The study found 40% will steal if there's little danger of getting caught. Only 30% won't steal at all, according to the study. What was a typical reason given for stealing when caught? All of the above.

8. As believers, how should we respond when someone is caught in a sin?

a) Galatians 6:1: Brothers, someone in your group might do something wrong. You who are spiritual should go to him and help make him right again. You should do this in a gentle way. But be careful! You might be tempted to sin, too.

As counselors, we should keep in mind that we might find ourselves in the same place as the fallen Christian someday. If we stay alert to our own vulnerability, it will help us maintain a steady and balanced approach to others. No one is immune from falling into sin. No believer grows in maturity to the point that he goes beyond susceptibility to temptation.

b) Matthew 18:15: "If your brother sins against you, go and tell him what he did wrong. Do this in private. If he listens to you, then you have helped him to be your brother again.

c) 2 Corinthians 2:7: But now you should forgive him and comfort him. This will keep him from having too much sadness and giving up completely.

d) 2 Timothy 2:25: The Lord's servant must gently teach those who do not agree with him. Maybe God will let them change their hearts so that they can accept the truth.

9. How would you counsel someone operating under the "I Won't Get Caught" thinking error?

I will let him know that, all things and everybody is not hidden from God. We are one day going to pay for our deeds, so it is better we change and follow God's instructions. King David said: "I fill all of heaven and earth," says the Lord. I cannot hide my guilt from you.

It can be discouraging because, when you directly confront a person with this thinking error, you'll seldom succeed in puncturing their ironclad belief system. Success at "getting away with murder" in the past has reinforced their confidence in continuing to commit crimes and not get caught. But we have to try, because it could be that not only their personal freedom from prison is at risk, but also their eternal destiny.

CHAPTER 21

I AM BASICALLY A GOOD PERSON

"I'm Basically a Good Person."

Most offenders see themselves as good human beings. No matter how long their list of crimes, no matter what suffering they have caused others, they will almost always claim that they are really good people. The criminal who operates under this thinking error will say things like, "In spite of my six arrests, I am basically a good person. I don't commit crimes all the time." "There's nothing wrong with me. All I did was sell a little dope." "I'm not a bad mother/father. My kids have never lived on the streets."

Some list their daily activities as evidence. They go to school or work most of the time, and take their family to church on Sundays. Others say they are good because they provide very well for their family. Some believe that, if God has blessed them with a special talent such as a musical ability, they must be basically good. Others figure that if they haven't hurt someone in the commission of their crimes, if they can pull off a robbery without pulling the trigger, they are "good people". A few believe that their violent acts were justified, that they did society a good service when they "offed" someone, and we should be thanking them instead of arresting them. Normally, criminals don't look in the mirror and see themselves as the villains that they really are.

And it's not just criminals who operate under this thinking error. There is a common perception that as long as a person leads a generally good life, they will get into heaven. You probably know people who say they are entitled to heaven because they read their Bible, go to church on Sundays, and live a moral life. And it's true - they haven't murdered or robbed anyone at gunpoint, they will give to charities now and then, and treat other people with respect. They honestly believe that hell is only for those few folks who have committed particularly evil acts.

This is as much a thinking error for you and I as it is for the criminal. Biblically speaking, when lined up against the plumb line of God's standards, no one is "good." To one degree or another, we all have fallen short of the glory of God (Romans 3:23). This does not mean that we are always actively engaged in committing crimes or have ever participated in a depraved act. But it does mean that in our very nature we are "fallen," in rebellion against God and incapable of saving ourselves.

a) How good is good enough to go to heaven? The Bible says God is good, and the Ten Commandments (Exodus 20:1-17) are His plumb line for measuring our personal goodness. Is there anyone who has perfectly kept all the commandments?

1. a) Is there anyone who has perfectly kept all the commandments? No

b) Explain your answer.: Apostle Paul said to the Church in Roman that: For all have sinned, and come short of the glory of God.

Only Jesus was sinless, and it is because Jesus was sinless that we have hope of an eternity in heaven. If Jesus were not sinless, there would be not have been a sacrifice worthy enough to bring before God for forgiveness of our sins. The sinless Christ's death on the cross at Calvary paid the full penalty for the sin of all who believe in Him.

2. a) If we trust in our own goodness to enter heaven, we are saying to God, "I should enter Heaven because I have earned my

way in." Is it possible to be good enough or to do enough good works to earn our way into heaven? No

b) Explain your answer. (Ephesians 2:8-9): 8 For it is by grace you have been saved, through faith—and this is not from yourselves, it is the gift of God— 9 not by works, so that no one can boast. Paul returns again to his theme of grace in this verse. Salvation's source is grace; the means of salvation is faith. We believe by faith to be saved (Romans 10:9), but would never choose to believe apart from the grace of God operating in our lives.

Only Christ's righteousness can satisfy God's righteousness.

3. In Philippians 3:9, Paul said that because he was in Him ..:
a) he (Paul) could renounce his own self
b) and live by the righteousness which is through faith in Christ
c) which is of God by faith

Amen! Our confidence at the Judgment Seat of Christ will not be in our works or how gooooood we were. It will be solely based on the finished, complete work of Christ. That work satisfies God completely. Our confidence is in Christ, not self.

4. Romans 11:6 explains this concept further. Grace and works don't go together.:
a) If our salvation is of grace, it cannot be of works
b) and if it is of works, it cannot be of Salvation must be by virtue of one or the other.: faith

I can't tell you how long, or how often, I planted and watered into my dad's salvation. The last time I talked to him about it, he was standing on a ladder fixing a ceiling fan. I figured he couldn't get away from me, so I laid it all out for him one more time. He said, "Honey, that's really a nice story. As a matter of fact, it's just too good to be true. I don't believe it." He thought the "by grace through faith" theory was too easy – there just had to be some works involved, somehow, some way.

I wasn't there when he was finally led to salvation while camping out with some friends. They must have been sitting around the campfire, and the conversation turned to the Lord. I wasn't there when he was baptized either, because his friends took care of that right then and there in the river by the campground where they were staying.

This happened one year before he died, and over that last year of his life, he always wanted to talk to me about the things of the Lord. What a joy that was. And I still weep over the day he asked Mike and I to meet him on a mountaintop in Oklahoma (a half-way point between the two of us), so he could pray the father's blessing over my life. When he asked that we come, we left immediately.

Be encouraged. We will never be able to measure what we have accomplished here on earth with regard to kingdom work. All we can do is keep on planting and watering and planting and watering, and know that God will give the increase in His perfect timing (1 Corinthians 3:6).

5. What is the ONLY way we can be justified?
We are justified through faith: Exhibit Romans 5:1 Therefore, since we have been justified through faith, we have peace with God through our Lord Jesus Christ,

6. The most important question we can ever ask in our lives is, "What must I do to be saved?" What is the answer?
a) First ... (1 John 1:9): we confess our sins,
b) Then ... (Acts 3:19): turn to God
c) Finally ... (Acts 16:31): Believe in the Lord Jesus, and you will be saved—you and your household

7. How would you counsel a person, offender or not, who says, "I'm basically a good person"?
Pray and then use the Word of God as follows: Romans 3:10-12 As it is written: "There is no one righteous, not even one; there is

no one who understands; there is no one who seeks God. All have turned away, they have together become worthless; there is no one who does good, not even one.

This is not just a criminal's thinking error. There are many law-abiding folks who fall into this trap as well.

My mother had always been a Catholic, and trusted in the fact that she was a good person for her entry into heaven. In the past, when I tried to talk to her about that, it created a wedge where she didn't even want to speak to me at all - one time for months. I finally got another chance when she was about 92. My mother woke me up at 5:45 in the morning, and told me she was scared. When I kept pressing her to tell me what she was afraid of, since I was right there to take care of her, she admitted that she was afraid to die. Oh, praise God.

We had a bit of a tussle over getting her to admit she is NOT perfectly good, that she HAS sinned. But after we got past that issue, I was able to explain the rest without so much argument. She let me lead her in prayer, and felt peace. The fear was gone. I know she believed me (and didn't just go along because she loves me) because afterwards she told me how smart I was and wondered how I knew all that and could explain it so well. I wanted to sing that old children's hymn Jesus Loves Me … but just the last line, "the Bible told me so." I just told her I read the Bible a lot.

CHAPTER 22

HE DID IT

"He Did It."

Cheaters always accuse others of cheating. Liars always accuse others of lying. Insecure people always try to make you feel insecure. And criminals like to accuse others of the very things they have done themselves. Their purpose in doing this is to deflect attention away from themselves and grab control over the situation.

Such a person has the bizarre ability to be able to make you feel guilty, to put you in the position where you feel the need to defend yourself for something you hadn't even thought of doing … when he/she knows very well he is the person who did it. He knows that while you are so busy standing up for yourself and trying to prove your own innocence, you will forget the real issue – the fact that the person pointing the finger at you should actually be pointing the finger at him or herself.

Being accused of a crime can have as much impact as a physical blow to the body, especially when the accusation is false. But it's all a game to the criminal mind. While sticking up for yourself, you will probably end up …

- feeling confused,
- feeling violated,
- feeling misunderstood,
- feeling unheard,
- feeling guilty,
- and feeling isolated.

If you catch such people in their lies, they neither win nor have control. So, they don't play fair. They do anything they can to come out victorious, by leaving everyone confused about who is the true guilty party, and thereby maintaining control. While you are feeling blindsided by the accusation, they are feeling smug and satisfied – seeing the drama they created that messed with your head, leaving you totally stressed out and frustrated.

Occasionally people aren't aware they're doing this. They may be unaware of the manipulative games they are playing, because liars will lie to themselves first before lying to others. When they lie to themselves long enough, the lie becomes the truth in their own minds.

1. There is a great power in the tongue and people have been falsely accusing others throughout the ages.:

a) How will the righteous be delivered from false accusations? (Proverbs 11:9): through knowledge the righteous escape.

How does he destroy others? He leads men to sin by pretending to have good intentions. He uses religion to get men to think well of him (Matthew 6:2, 5, 16; 23:14, 25, 27). He speaks of loving the Lord but lives for himself, which undermines the faith of those watching.

The just man is saved from the hypocrite by knowing the truth, which gives him the wisdom and understanding to reject the hypocrite's ideas. He is able to discern the heresies or lies of the hypocrite and ignore his pompous pretensions.

b) In Isaiah 54:17, the Lord spoke to Israel and told her not to be concerned about the lies being told about her because …: No weapon that is formed against thee shall prosper; and every tongue that shall rise against thee in judgment thou shalt condemn. This is the heritage of the servants of the Lord, and their righteousness is of Me," saith the Lord.

Satan leaves no stone unturned against the Church of God. And one of his best weapons is the tongue. But we can trust in the Lord's triumph over Satan's lies.

c) When we are persecuted, insulted, and lied about for the sake of Jesus, we will be … (Matthew 5:11): happy. Exhibit: "People will say bad things about you and hurt you. They will lie and say all kinds of evil things about you because you follow me. But when they do these things to you, you are happy.

Here Jesus brings insults and spoken lies into the sphere of persecution. We cannot limit our idea of persecution to only physical opposition or torture.

e) Will it help the situation if we go around spreading lies about the person who has falsely accused us? No
f) Explain your answer. (Romans 12:19; Luke 6:27): Pursuant to Romans 12:19: for it is written, Vengeance is mine; I will repay, saith the Lord.

A person who trusts in God won't think it's necessary to get even with someone. They will leave the issue of vengeance up to God.

2. Our primary spiritual enemy and accuser is Satan.: a) What trait is at the root of his character? (John 8:44): Lies. Exhibit: there is no truth in him. for he is a liar, and the father of it.

Jesus gives us some insight into the character of Satan. The lie is core to the devil's character, and he is the deceiver most dangerous of all – a deceiver who has deceived himself.

b) What is the first lie Satan said that we know about? Thou shall not die when you eat the fruit of knowledge of good and evil.

c) How does he disguise himself so he can more easily deceive people? (2 Corinthians 11:14): transformed himself into an angel of light.

In the same way that Satan may appear as an angel of light, so false teachers may have a "good" appearance and a charismatic personality. Paul is showing the Corinthian Christians how foolish it is to rely on image and outward appearances.

d) What does Satan spend his time doing?

i) 1 Peter 5:8: walketh about, seeking whom he may devour:

A roaring lion intimidates by his roar and Satan intimidates by fear. He strikes fear into weak Christians because that will intimidate them from a life of faith. As a lion in the wild chases a herd of gazelles and runs down the weak of the herd, so Satan usually catches weak Christians first because he freezes them in fear. Fear incapacitates us from moving ahead with our Christian walk.

In addition, like a lion, Satan uses stealth. He stalks every Christian. He is always seeking opportunities to undermine our Christian walk. He is constantly on the prowl. He is not omnipresent for he can only be in one place at a time. However, he has a massive infrastructure of emissaries (demons) who do his bidding. They seek to deceive every one of us.

ii) Revelations 12:10: accuses us before our God Day and night.

e) Who are some others that we have on record as being falsely accused by Satan?
i) Zechariah 3:1-2: Joshua
ii) Job 2:1-6: Job

f) How can we defend ourselves against the schemes, lies, and accusations of Satan? (Ephesians 6:11): We have to put on the whole armor of God, that ye may be able to stand against the wiles of the devil.

The believer is responsible to put on his own spiritual armor. The Greek indicates that we are to put on spiritual armor with a sense of urgency. The believer needs to decisively put on God's armor. The challenge is to accept God's provision for his protection from Satan.

g) Satan works on earth to turn God's children against God and in heaven to turn God against His children. But he doesn't stand a chance of succeeding because ... (Romans 8:31): Because God is for us. Exhibit: What shall we then say to these things? If God be for us, who can be against us?

3. How would you counsel a person who, when backed into a corner, tends to point the finger at others, and accuse them of the very thing he/she has done?

Pray with the person and read Bible verses to guide him/her. Example: The accuser of our brethren who accuses them before our God Day and night (Revelation 12:10) So, I will encourage the person to start be responsible for his/her own actions and stop pointing fingers

CHAPTER 23

I DIDN'T MEAN TO

"I Didn't Mean To."

You have probably heard it said, "That was an accident. I didn't mean to do it." This is a defense that felons might actually believe themselves. For example, if someone was injured or killed in the commission of their crime, they may offer that excuse, but weren't they aware something like that could happen beforehand? You may also hear …

- I didn't do it on purpose.
- I wasn't trying to …
- It was a mistake.
- Oops! That wasn't supposed to happen.
- I only meant to ...
- I didn't know that would upset you.
- It just slipped out.
- That's not what I meant.
- I didn't plan it that way.

But how is that possible? If we didn't mean what we said, or didn't mean what we did, why did we do it? And then why make up such a ridiculous excuse? I believe that excuse is offered because it turns the table on the accuser. Now you look like the bad guy if you don't say, "Oh, that's all right. I understand." It's actually another way to grab a position of power in a potentially explosive situation.

Criminals aren't the only ones who fall back on this excuse. Let's say that a man made an extramarital sexual connection on his business trip. If his spouse finds out, the first thing you might hear him say is: "Oh honey, it didn't mean anything. It was just sex." That excuse is supposed to take all of the bite out of his spouse's righteous anger, and get her to calm down. Or, imagine he got drunk and said some abusive things to her. Later he apologized saying, "I was just drunk, baby. I didn't mean to hurt your feelings." Or, he got really angry, blew his stack and later said, "I was just mad, sweetheart. I didn't mean any of it." Such a lame excuse actually makes it worse.

Bottom line? We say what we mean, mean what we say, and we intended to do what we did. We might try to imply certain actions or words were unintentional, but the Bible says they are always intentional. Proverbs 23:7 says, "As a man is in his heart, so is he." Whether in town or out, whether sober or drunk, whether angry or not - what is really in our hearts is what will show up in our words and actions.

1. Will making excuses for our sins ever work with God?

Proverbs 21:2 says that we may deceive ourselves with our excuses, to justify remaining in sin and committing more sins. But God looks beyond the excuses and sees the very root of our sins, our heart

Do criminals think God does not see the truth in their hearts? He fills heaven and earth (Jeremiah 23:23-24)! He knows the thoughts and intents of every heart: all things are naked and open to His holy eyes (Hebrews 4:12-13). Our most intimate and secret fantasies are exposed (Proverbs 5:20-21; Ecclesiastes 12:14). The Jews found Jesus' perception to be supernatural more than once (Matthew 9:3-4; 12:25).

2. What could help you determine if the excuse given is the truth or a lie? (Luke 6:43-45): A good person has good things saved up in his heart. And so he brings good things out of his heart.

This fruit is the inevitable result and revelation of who we really are.

3. Read Luke 14:16-20. Just like today, to not attend a banquet when one had previously accepted was a grave breach of social etiquette and an insult to the host. The host had planned the banquet based on the number of guests invited. Once the RSVPs were in, and the host had determined how many guests would be there, he had known exactly how many animals should be killed and cooked.:

Luke 14:16-20

16 Then He said to him, "A certain man gave a great supper and invited many, 17 and sent his servant at supper time to say to those who were invited, 'Come, for all things are now ready.' 18 But they all with one accord began to make excuses. The first said to him, 'I have bought a piece of ground, and I must go and see it. I ask you to have me excused.' 19 And another said, 'I have bought five yoke of oxen, and I am going to test them. I ask you to have me excused.' 20 Still another said, 'I have married a wife, and therefore I cannot come.'

a) What were the excuses people gave for not attending the banquet?

i): I have bought a field, and I go out and see it;

ii): 'I have bought five yoke of oxen, and I must go to examine them; I pray you, have me excused.'

The first two excuses had to do with material things, and were foolish excuses. Only a fool first buys a piece of land, and then goes to check it. Only a fool buys ten oxen and is only interested in testing them after the purchase. When we buy something new, we are almost always preoccupied by it. Preoccupation with material things and experiences is a common excuse for not following Jesus.

iii): I have married a wife, and therefore I cannot come.'

The third excuse had to do with a man who put his family before everything. The best thing we can show to our family is that Jesus Christ is first in our lives.

b) Likewise, people offer excuses today for not accepting Jesus' invitation to be saved. If Christianity is so true and so good, why don't more embrace it? Why give excuses instead of accepting Jesus' invitation? (Thought question): Some will say, I am a good person and a member of Church. Others will say I am a Christian.

They like their secret, habitual sin. They don't want to give up time or resources to support the church. They know too many hypocrites that attend church. Someone at the church hurt their feelings once. But these excuses are just a thin veil hiding the fact that some people just don't want to accept Jesus. They like the status quo. If they accept Jesus, they might not have their weekends to themselves any more – to do whatever they want to do. They don't want to be bothered with going to church, attending or leading small groups, helping out by serving at church services.
They're sure not seeing the big picture with their eternal destiny at stake.

4. Leviticus 4 takes into account the likelihood that people will do things that are wrong without knowing it or without meaning to do wrong.:

a) What if the priest sins unintentionally through ignorance? (vs. 2-3): If so, he has brought guilt on the people. So, he must offer a young bull to the Lord. It must have nothing wrong with it. This will be a sin offering for the sin he has done.

b) What if the entire congregation sins unintentionally? (vs. 13-14): When they learn about the sin they have done, a young bull must be offered. It is a sin offering for the whole nation. They must bring it and give it before the Meeting Tent.

The idea is not so much of an accidental sin, but of a sin committed by a person who basically loves God. The contrast to an unintentional sin is to sin presumptuously (Numbers 15:30). Literally, this was "to sin with a high hand."

c) In the verses above, we see that even inadvertent, unwitting sin defiles us. What if we continue sinning after we have learned the truth? (Hebrews 10:26): If we decide to go on sinning after we have learned the truth, there is no longer any sacrifice for sins.

To sin willfully is defined in Hebrews 10:29. It speaks of someone who has trampled the Son of God underfoot, counted the blood of the covenant by which he was sanctified a common thing, and insulted the Spirit of grace. It is a knowing, deliberate rejection of Jesus' great work for us on the cross.

5. What about God? Does He ever look down from heaven and say, "Oops! I didn't mean for that to happen"?

a) Jeremiah 29:11 tells us that God has plans for us. Describe His plans.: I say this because I know what I have planned for you," says the Lord. "I have good plans for you. I don't plan to hurt you. I plan to give you hope and a good future.

It is one of Satan's favorite deceptions - to rob God's people of their sense of His future and a hope for them. But these were God's thoughts toward Israel under the Old Covenant. And His thoughts are no less favorable to those who come to Him in faith, through the Messiah, in the New Covenant.

b) But not everything that happens is God's will or plan for our life. For example, it is not God's will that ... (2 Peter 3:9), but some have in the past and certainly more will in the future.: The Lord is not slow in doing what he promised—the way some people understand slowness. But God is being patient with you. He does not want anyone to be lost. He wants everyone to change his heart and life.

6. Then why do bad things happen to good people? a) First of all, we need to be clear - there are no "good" people. The

Bible makes it abundantly clear that all of us are tainted by and infected with (Ecclesiastes 7:20; Romans 3:23; 1 John 1:8; Romans 3:10-18): Sin

Not only have we all sinned, but we have also fallen FAR short of God's standard. No one can measure up to the absolute perfection of God's righteousness.

b) After we become believers, we may bring fewer problems down on ourselves, but Jesus clearly warned us ...: Jesus Christ says, "Watch therefore, for you do not know what hour your Lord is coming." He repeats this statement again in Matthew 25:13.

c) But for those who love God ... (Romans 8:28): We know that in everything God works for the good of those who love him. They are the people God called, because that was his plan.

7. The whole story of Ruth, from her husband and father-in-law dying and her staying with her mother-in-law Naomi, seemed to be an account of one disaster after another - until she went to the field and met and married Boaz. How did all this work together for good in God's plans?

(Matthew 1:5-6): Through that Jesus was born. This is the family history of Jesus Christ. He came from the family of David. David came from the family of Abraham.

Ruth became the great-grandmother of Israel's king David, demonstrating that a foreigner could be completely assimilated into God's people and become His instrument for redemptive purpose. Jesus' descent from David's family in both blood through His mother, Mary, and legal kinship through His father, Joseph, gave Him legitimacy as Messiah to Israel among His first Jewish followers. Jesus' descent from Ruth made it clear that the Messiah would redeem all humanity, not only the Jews.

Clearly, the book of Ruth represents an early sign that the Messiah would liberate all of humankind, not solely Jews, and that Gentiles would join God's community of redeemed people in the mission of restoring God's lost children back into full relationship with Him.

8. Consider this account in Acts 28. First, Paul was on a ship for Rome that sank in a storm off Malta. Next Paul got bitten by a viper. Then, the father of the ruler of the island got sick while they were there and Paul was able to heal him. How did all this work together for good? Paul was able to preach in Rome under guard.

As Paul headed to Rome, the sea, the soldiers, and the snake all threatened his life. But God delivered him from them all. Through Paul, God shows that a believer endeavoring to fulfill God's will cannot be stopped – even when all kinds of difficulty may come in the way. Also, I think we can see from Paul's unselfish example that, even as we approach the end of our lives (and Paul knew when he got to Rome that would mean the end), God still has plenty of work for us to do.

9. How would you counsel the person who habitually falls back on the excuse, "I didn't mean to"?

Remind the person what Christ says in Revelation 16:15, "Blessed is he who watches..." This means far more than just looking for signs in the heavens for Christ's return. We need to keep an eye on events in the world around us and most importantly, be on guard against religious deception.

CHAPTER 24

I WAS DESPERATE

"I Was Desperate."

It's a common belief that if you do the crime, you should do the time. And why not? If you have made the decision to commit a crime — no matter what that crime is — then you should be punished for the pain, suffering, and financial loss you have caused victims and their families. But there is a disproportionate number of crimes being committed today by single mothers recently. These women are resorting to crime just to provide basic needs for their family, and crimes of this type are now being referred to as "crimes of desperation."

As the slumping economy has taken its toll on people's lives, police departments all across the country are reporting a jump in crimes of desperation including robberies, burglaries, car thefts and shoplifting. They're seeing homeless transients who are sleeping on park benches, hungry, and cold trying to get arrested - simply as a way to come in out of the cold and get a few free meals. They're seeing an increase in "white collar" crime by people with relatively easy access to enormous amounts of money, who feel compelled to embezzle funds to clear up a pressing financial obligation.

Another common scenario is the drug addict who is in desperate need of money for his next fix. He decides the quickest way to get money is to hold up a convenience store. As he's demanding cash from the check-out clerk, a customer confronts him and, feeling threatened, he shoots the customer impulsively.

We've all seen TV shows where a compulsive gambler owes a large amount of money to some organized crime organization. He's been warned that he better pay off the ever-growing loan or get his knees broken. So, he kills his wife or burns down his own house for the insurance money.

These are sobering times that we live in today. Many people have lost their jobs and can't find another one. Others are underemployed and are just barely making it. The unemployment rate is soaring, the stock market is highly volatile, and famine is spreading worldwide. People who commit crimes of desperation are in crisis mode. They feel they have run out of options. They commit crimes to resolve what seems to be an unresolvable predicament.

The spiritual issue with committing a crime in a desperate situation is that we are taking matters into our own hands, instead of trusting God to bring us through.

1. What can we do when our backs are against the wall and there is nowhere to turn?

a) God's desire is that we ... (Psalm 50:15). Psalm 50:15

¹⁵ Call upon Me in the day of trouble;

I will deliver you, and you shall glorify Me."

This verse contains three parts, and all three are about prayer.

1. The first is a command, "… call upon me in the day of trouble."
2. The second part of the verse is the promise, "… and I will deliver you."
3. And the third part is our response, "… and you will glorify me."

Sadly, this is often the forgotten part of prayer. Prayer is not just a way to get our needs met or our rescue made possible, though that happens. Prayer is about praising God. God could and does supply our needs even when we don't pray. But He prefers that we pray, because then we are more likely to recognize His hand of provision

b) Because He loves us, when we call on God, He will ... (Psalm 91:14-16).

God said They will call me, and I will answer them.

c) 1 Peter 5:7 says that when we are anxious, we should Give all your worries to him, because he cares for you.

The Greek used the word "casting" to refer a man who carried a heavy burden and threw it up on a camel's back. I always think of the discus thrower in the Olympics - the way he throws that heavy disc with all his might, as far as possible. The pressures and the burdens of your life are so heavy and difficult, and Jesus wants you to catapult them right out of your life and into His. He has promised to take care of everything for us.

2. Some find it difficult to trust God when everything seems to be caving in around them. How do the following verses reassure us?

a) Isaiah 41:13 For I, the Lord thy God, will hold thy right hand, saying unto thee, 'Fear not; I will help thee.'

b) Proverbs 3:5-6 Remember the Lord in everything you do.   And he will give you success.

This is the true basis of wisdom. Reject your own ideas, and instead trust God's inspired revelation and sovereign providence to save you in your time of trouble. If you choose to go your own way against His will, you will suffer.

c) Romans 8:31 So, what should we say about this? If God is for us, then no one can defeat us

Because God is "for us," no power — including Satan and all his hosts — can prevail against the believer. All our adversity is under God's control. God will always go to battle for us, and so nothing can stop our future from happening. As long as we live, God will be "for us."

This promise allows us to face our problems with a divine viewpoint. We can deal with pressure when we trust in God's providential care for us.

3. Because we have a High Priest who is both omnipotent and compassionate, what attitude should we have when we come before His throne with a desperate request? (Hebrews 4:16)

Let us, then, feel free to come before God's throne. Here there is grace. And we can receive mercy and grace to help us when we need it.

4. The Bible has recorded seven separate occasions when Saul attempted to kill David (1 Samuel 18:11; 1 Samuel 18:25; 1 Samuel 19:9-10; 1 Samuel 19:11, 15; 1 Samuel 20:31-33; 1 Samuel 23:9; 1 Samuel 23:25-26). This was surely a desperate situation for David.

David had at least two opportunities to kill King Saul, recorded in 1 Samuel 24 and 1 Samuel 26, yet both times, David refused to kill Saul himself and David refused to allow his warriors to kill King Saul.

Why did David refuse to commit this crime of desperation?

a) 1 Samuel 24:6: "May the Lord keep me from doing such a thing to my master! Saul is the Lord's appointed king. I should not do anything against him, because he is the Lord's appointed king!"

b) 1 Samuel 26:9: David said to Abishai, "Don't kill Saul! No one can harm the Lord's appointed king and still be innocent!

David considered Saul's life precious and of tremendous value. Though David had killed men in war, he would not kill Saul (1 Samuel 26:24). David had great faith in God's plan and timing. As long as God wanted Saul to be king, David would wait. He would not take matters into his own hands.

5. If a single mother shoplifts school supplies and school clothes for her children, should she receive a lighter sentence than

someone who shoplifts for the thrill? (Thought question – answers will vary)

All sins are the same before God. James 2:10 where it says, "If you have committed one sin you are guilty of all." Which seems to mean that, whether small sin or big sin, I'm totally guilty of all the commandments.

It can be dangerous to attempt to list sins according to their degree of seriousness. In one sense, all sins are equal in that they all separate us from God. The Bible's statement, "For the wages of sin is death …" (Romans 6:23), applies to all sin, whether in thought, word, or deed.

At the same time, it seems obvious that some sins are worse than others in both motivation and effects, and should be judged accordingly. Stealing a loaf of bread is vastly different than exterminating a million people. Sins may also differ at their root. However, whether our sins are relatively small or great, they will place us in hell apart from God's grace. The good news is that Jesus paid the penalty for our sins and the sins of the whole world at the Cross.

6. How would you counsel a person who is considering committing a crime, because he is in a real desperate situation?

Pursuant to Isaiah 59:1-2 Behold, the Lord's hand is not shortened, that it cannot save, or his ear dull, that it cannot hear; but your iniquities have made a separation between you and your God, and your sins have hidden his face from you so that he does not hear.

Remind the person to read 1 Corinthians 10:13 KJV There hath no temptation taken you but such as is common to man: but God is faithful, who will not suffer you to be tempted above that ye are able; but will with the temptation also make a way to escape, that ye may be able to bear it.

7. a) Finally, in conclusion, is there any reasonable excuse we can offer God that will justify our committing a crime?

a) No, there is none.

b) Pursuant to Isaiah 59:1-2 Behold, the Lord's hand is not shortened, that it cannot save, or his ear dull, that it cannot hear; but your iniquities have made a separation between you and your God, and your sins have hidden his face from you so that he does not hear. I will remind the person to read 1 Corinthians 10:13 KJV There hath no temptation taken you but such as is common to man: but God is faithful, who will not suffer you to be tempted above that ye are able; but will with the temptation also make a way to escape, that ye may be able to bear it.

Shalom,

Dr. Maxwell Shimba

THE END

ACKNOWLEDGEMENTS

My special thanks to my dear wife Zippy, my sons Mel, and Ian for their constant love and support.

My thanks to my late Father Reuben Shimba for his consultations and editorial work in the preparation of this manuscript.

I also wish to thank my loving mother Lois for her prayers, which are a constant source of strength and encouragement to me. My appreciation to my dedicated staff for their assistance with this project.

ABOUT THE AUTHOR

Dr. Maxwell Shimba: A Biography

Dr. Maxwell Shimba is a multifaceted individual whose life journey has been marked by a deep commitment to the fields of restorative justice, literature, religious scholarship, and education. His remarkable contributions span a diverse range of endeavors, making him a prominent figure in these domains.

Restorative Justice Advocate:

Dr. Maxwell Shimba's passion for justice is evident in his role as a dedicated Restorative Justice practitioner. With a profound understanding of this transformative approach to justice, he has actively worked to promote healing, reconciliation, and rehabilitation in the face of conflicts and wrongdoing.

Prolific Author:

An accomplished author, Dr. Shimba has penned numerous books that traverse various disciplines. His literary repertoire includes works on law, religion, finance, and other pertinent subjects. Through his writings, he has not only shared knowledge but also inspired and enlightened countless readers.

Bible Scholar:

Dr. Maxwell Shimba's deep reverence for the Bible is reflected in his status as a Bible scholar. His rigorous study of scripture has allowed him to unravel its profound teachings and share them with others, enriching their understanding of faith and spirituality.

Founder of USA Theological University:

In his quest to further theological education, Dr. Shimba founded the USA Theological University in the vibrant city of Orlando, Florida. This institution stands as a testament to his commitment to nurturing the intellectual and spiritual growth of students, imparting knowledge, and fostering a deeper connection with matters of faith.

Teacher and Preacher:

Dr. Maxwell Shimba is not merely an academic but also a dedicated teacher and preacher. Through his teachings and sermons, he imparts wisdom, guidance, and spiritual insights to those who seek a deeper understanding of their faith and the principles that guide their lives.

Dr. Maxwell Shimba's life journey embodies a profound dedication to the principles of justice, faith, education, and the written word. His work continues to impact and influence individuals across various walks of life, making him a beacon of knowledge, inspiration, and positive change in the world.

SHIMBA
PUBLISHING

www.ingramcontent.com/pod-product-compliance
Lightning Source LLC
Chambersburg PA
CBHW061254120726

48001CB00001B/302